YORK NO

General Editors: Profes:
of Stirling) & Professor
University of Beirut)

John Milton

SELECTED POEMS

Notes by Peter Bayley

MA (OXFORD)
Professor Emeritus of the University of St Andrews

LONGMAN
YORK PRESS

YORK PRESS
Immeuble Esseily, Place Riad Solh, Beirut.

LONGMAN GROUP UK LIMITED
Longman House, Burnt Mill, Harlow,
Essex CM20 2JE, England
and Associated Companies throughout the world.

© Librairie du Liban 1982

First published 1982
Reprinted 1989

ISBN 0-582-02275-4

Produced by Longman Group (FE) Ltd.
Printed in Hong Kong

Contents

Part 1: Introduction   *page* 5

  Milton's life and times   5

  A note on the text   13

Part 2: Summaries   14

  'On the Morning of Christ's Nativity'   14

  'L'Allegro' and 'Il Penseroso'   21

  Comus   28

  'Lycidas'   38

  Some sonnets   45

  Samson Agonistes   55

Part 3: Commentary   65

  'On the Morning of Christ's Nativity'   65

  'L'Allegro' and 'Il Penseroso'   68

  Comus   69

  'Lycidas'   75

  Samson Agonistes   80

Part 4: Hints for study   87

  General points   87

  Preparing for examinations   88

  Writing essays and examinations   89

  Specimen questions and answers   90

Part 5: Suggestions for further reading   97

The author of these notes   99

Part 1

Introduction

Milton's life and times

John Milton was born in London on 9 December 1608, the son of John Milton, a well-to-do scrivener. By this time, a scrivener was more than simply a copier; he was a lawyer and law-stationer. The poet's father was musical, and wrote some songs and psalm tunes which survive; and the younger Milton later wrote, in *The Second Defence of the People of England* (1654), that his father had encouraged him in:

> the pursuits of literature; and my appetite for knowledge was so voracious that from twelve years of age, I hardly ever left my studies or went to bed before midnight . . . I had from my first years by the ceaseless diligence and care of my father . . . been exercised to the tongues, and some sciences, as my age would suffer, by sundry masters and teachers, both at home and at the schools.

The young John Milton learned Latin, Greek, Hebrew, Italian and French. He was also interested and became knowledgeable in natural history, geography and history as well, of course, as literature, both ancient and modern. He had a private tutor at first, then went to one of the great City schools of London, St Paul's. Here he studied Latin and also a great deal of Renaissance poetry and especially that of Edmund Spenser. From there he went up to Christ's College, Cambridge, at the age of seventeen, in 1625.

That year, 1625, was the year in which King Charles I succeeded his father, James I. Both kings were unwise and unpopular. James I had the double difficulty of being Scottish, not English, and of having to succeed the brilliant and powerful Queen Elizabeth I, who had reigned from 1558 until 1603 and had left England confident, powerful, and, despite continuing differences about religion, more united than it had ever been. Furthermore, James was autocratic and extravagant without having his predecessor's ability. He determined to be an 'absolute' ruler, and tried to bring everything under his own control, but failed. Parliament resisted him, notably when he attempted to gain control of the judiciary, over finance and over the Church. He was opposed in the first two by Parliament, and in the latter also by the 'Puritan' movement both within the Church and outside it. This was not a recognisable organisation pursuing one approved policy. The Puritans agreed on the need for reform of the Church of England and opposition to the King and to the whole Church hierarchy of archbishops and bishops, through which the King sought, as Head of the English Church, to control it. (The King controlled the Church chiefly because it was he who appointed the bishops.) The Puritans strove for a purer, simpler, more austere form of worship, and a simpler, more democratic Church organisation. They hoped also to free the Church of abuses, extravagance and worldliness. Puritan feeling had been growing for at least forty years before Charles's accession, and Cambridge in Milton's time was, as it had long been, the centre of the reforming Puritan movement. (Milton's admired predecessor, the Elizabethan Edmund Spenser, also a Londoner and a Cambridge man, had strong Puritan connections and affinities.) Milton at Christ's College must have been fully aware of, if not actually involved in the movement, and from the age of about thirty until his death he was of the Puritan persuasion. For a vital part of his life during the Puritan Commonwealth, he was actively engaged at the very centre.

He graduated Bachelor of Arts in 1629. By that time he had written 'At a Solemn Music' and 'On the Morning of Christ's Nativity' in English and a great deal more in Latin. After taking his Master of Arts degree in 1632, he settled at Horton, a Buckinghamshire village near Slough where his father had retired. He had decided not to enter the Church. He was already disenchanted with and critical of the Church, which he thought 'tyranny had invaded . . . he who would take Orders must subscribe slave'. King Charles I was attempting the same absolutist policy as his father, and the Church was firmly in his grasp through his Archbishop, Laud, though opposition was stirring fast. Being unwilling to become a priest, Milton was disqualified from a Fellowship (a Fellow is a senior full teaching member of an Oxford or Cambridge college). His independent, even rebellious nature would not have fitted him for the discipline of the Church. For five years, after finishing at Cambridge, 'on my father's estate I enjoyed an interval of uninterrupted leisure, which I entirely devoted to the perusal of the Greek and Latin classics'. 'Entirely' cannot have been quite the right word; he also read widely in Italian literature, in philosophy and in history, and studied mathematics and music 'in which I at that time found a source of pleasure and amusement'. He was making himself the most learned of all English poets. He wrote some poetry: 'L'Allegro' and 'Il Penseroso'; the fragmentary 'Arcades', and *Comus*, and at the end of this period, in 1638, the elegy 'Lycidas' commemorating Edward King, a contemporary of his and later a Fellow of Christ's, who was drowned at sea. In this poem, for the first time he made a powerful attack on the state of the Church, which King had been intending to enter (see the notes on 'Lycidas', p. 42, and Commentary, p. 77). It is the first glimpse of Milton's interest in matters of public and general importance.

In the same year, in April 1638, he began a fourteen-month visit to Europe, spending most of the time in Italy. But while he was 'peacefully travelling for culture', as he called it, affairs at home had developed rapidly. The King was preparing to invade Scotland, after the Scots at the Glasgow Assembly in November 1637 had defied him, deposed their bishops, annulled all forms and ordinances of Episcopacy and re-established Presbyterianism (a Calvinistic reformed Church without a hierarchy of archbishops, bishops, and so on). Far from receiving support and votes of money for this purpose, he met only resistance and opposition; in any case, he had been ruling without Parliament for nine years. In 1639, with a disaffected and disorganised army he faced the Scots near Berwick-on-Tweed, realised the hopeless situation he was in and patched up an agreement with them. In 1640 he summoned Parliament, for the first time for eleven years, but dissolved it after three weeks because the members of Parliament demanded immediate redress of their grievances. Their sympathies at this time, being in general anti-episcopal, were largely with the Scottish Presbyterians.

All through this period, it is almost impossible to disentangle religion from political issues. For Milton's prose and poetry, from this time on, the same can be said. When he is writing about freedom, the ostensible subject may be religious, but it is also political and general. When he is writing about political rights he is also thinking of religious toleration. When he discusses the individual's claims to liberty of conscience, the whole struggle of the Puritans in religion and the Parliamentary party in politics is also in his mind.

Milton returned from Italy in August 1639 ('for I thought it base to be travelling at my ease abroad . . . while my fellow-citizens were fighting for liberty at home'), at the time of the so-called First Bishop's War, and settled in London, taking his widowed sister's two fatherless boys as pupils, and later a few other boys of good family. A year later, the Second Bishops' War again resulted in discomfiture and humiliation for the King, who was worsted at Newburn-on-Tyne in August 1640 and again had to sue for an armistice. After this he had to summon Parliament again. The members of Parliament this time realised their power. They defied the King in several ways, refusing to vote money, impeaching and sentencing to death the King's loyal chief supporter Strafford, and later arresting Archbishop Laud. The following year, 1641, they asserted their strength, showing that they and not the King were the strongest power in the country. They secured Parliamentary rights of the greatest importance, making it impossible for a King to rule for long without a Parliament and denying a king the right to dissolve Parliament without consent. They also moved in the matter of religion, pressing for the abolition, 'root and branch', of bishops. Obviously, the country's opposition to a king who wished to rule like a tyrant was coming to a head. Every attempt to punish the Scots for their defiant Presbyterianism, every attempt to reinforce the power of the episcopal Church of England, every fresh demand for more money, every interference with Parliament, strengthened the opposition to him.

The Civil War became inevitable when in January 1642 the King tried in person to arrest in the House of Commons (the second or lower chamber of Parliament, the other being the House of Lords) five members of Parliament whom he had accused of complicity with the Scots in the previous year. This attempt to force his will deeply shocked Parliament, and the City of London, and alienated many of his own supporters. In the following months, the opposition set about forming an army and the King made his own preparations. He set up his standard on 22 August 1642 at Nottingham, summoning all loyal subjects to support him against a rebellious Parliament.

In the period between Milton's return from the Continent and the outbreak of the Civil War, two significant developments in his life occurred. He started writing tracts or pamphlets attacking the Church and pressing for the abolition of episcopacy. Like many others, he no longer believed in the possibility of decent churchmanship, let alone religious liberty, under episcopacy. *Of Reformation in England*, *Of Prelatical Episcopacy*, and *Animadversions upon the Remonstrant's Defence* were published anonymously in 1641. They all supported the Parliamentarians who called for the pulling-up of bishops 'root and branch', and attacked also the liturgy, clerical pomp and dress, and the old prayer-book, calling for a return to faithful understanding of the Scriptures as the only basis of religious life. (This ignored the fact that there were many hundreds of sincere and virtuous priests in the Church of England.) The last, *The Reason of Church Government urg'd against Prelaty*, published under his own name in February 1642, more definitely shows his alignment with the Presbyterian cause (which before long he came to think itself too tyrannical and intolerant). So John Milton declared his allegiance in the conflict between King and Parliament, between Anglicanism and Puritan dissent, which month by month during these years was gathering momentum.

The other significant development was in his personal life. In May or June 1642, at the age of thirty-three, he married a young girl of sixteen. Mary Powell's family was from Oxford, indeed near the home of Milton's long-dead Catholic grandfather. It was a family to which he had lent money. More significant, and strangely, it was a Royalist family. Within a month or so, the young girl left him and returned to 'the much Company and Joviality' of her family home from her new husband's intellectualism and austerity. The speedy breakdown of their marriage may have been caused by the approaching dangers of the now certain civil war, but more likely was chiefly the result of disharmony or incompatibility. It prompted the writing of tracts in which he examined the whole subject of marriage and divorce and called for a relaxation of the laws governing divorce. *The Doctrine and Discipline of Divorce* was written and published in 1643, after the outbreak of the Civil War, *The Judgement of Martin Bucer concerning Divorce* in 1644, *Tetrachordon* and *Colasterion* in 1645. Mary Powell returned home in midsummer 1642; the Civil War began in August; it would have been difficult for her to return from Royalist Oxfordshire to a Parliamentarian London about to be besieged, but it does not seem as if she tried to or wished to.

Both sets of pamphlets expose two strong elements in Milton's nature: the love of liberty and a stubborn, rebellious will. There were also a considerable degree of self-interest, of selfishness even, and of what today would be called male chauvinism, in the case of the divorce pamphlets, but also a serious consideration of fundamental principles. Both sets of writing got him into some trouble, for he had not complied with a recent wartime ordinance, of June 1643, requiring publications to be licensed and registered. That ordinance led indirectly to the writing of Milton's greatest prose work, *Areopagitica*, published in 1644. More than a plea for what its sub-title called 'the Liberty of Unlicenc'd Printing', it is a moving and powerful argument for intellectual freedom; 'who ever knew truth put to the worse, in a free and open encounter?' *Areopagitica* nobly argues a noble cause. The abuse and rancour of some of the other pamphlets is here replaced by dignified eloquence.

For ten years or more, the Presbyterian part of the Puritan opposition – believing in democratic Church rule and organisation by the congregations – had become even stronger. If Anglicanism were to be abolished, it could be replaced at that time only by Presbyterianism. Furthermore, from at least the middle of 1643, Presbyterianism, which had received further encouragement from the fact that Scotland had thrown off episcopacy and was firmly Presbyterian, actually dominated Parliament. Milton had by this time come to deplore and oppose both their attempts to limit freedom of speech and their demand for uniformity, which amounted to limitation of freedom of worship. Liberty and toleration seemed in danger, even if not to the same extent as under the King's autocratic rule. So Milton attached himself to the Independents, approving of their stand in Parliament. Their Parliamentary leader was Oliver Cromwell, Member of Parliament for Huntingdon and later Cambridge, and the Army on the whole was of their persuasion.

The would-be poet was now fully engaged in public events. His *Poems* – the 'Nativity Ode', 'L'Allegro', 'Il Penseroso', *Comus*, 'Lycidas', some sonnets and a few other pieces – appeared in 1646. The work contained nothing, except three sonnets and some Latin poems, that had been written since 1637 or 1638. His pen had been fully engaged in prose controversy. Yet he was thinking all the time of his life-long project for a great literary work, and he made lists of possible subjects, some to be in dramatic, some in epic form. In the same year, 1645, his young wife Mary returned to him, presumably after the defeat of the Royalist cause, and their first daughter was born in July 1646.

The brilliant leadership of Cromwell and the generalship of Sir Thomas Fairfax, with the fundamental strength and the great resources of the rebellious party, led gradually to the overpowering of the Royalist forces. The King was heavily defeated at Naseby, in the Midland county of Northamptonshire, in June 1645, and that marked the end of the war, although it took some months before all resistance everywhere was wiped out. It was an uneasy, and, as it turned out, impermanent peace, lasting less than three years. For two significant developments occurred: the Cromwellian Army and the Parliament came to be in opposition to each other, and the King brought the Scots in on his side. The quarrel of the Army and Parliament was over the matter of religious toleration, which the Presbyterian majority in Parliament would deny. The King tried to play one off against the other, and then he entered into a secret agreement with the Scots. In April 1648 a Scottish army crossed the border, and the Second Civil War began. In August they were roundly beaten at Preston in Lancashire by Cromwell, and by the end of that month the war was over. The Independents of the Army were now the dominant force; in December the Independents gained control of Parliament by excluding ninety-six of their Presbyterian opponents. In January 1649 this Parliament, having resolved to bring the King to Justice, declared that the Members of the House of Commons formed the supreme authority in England. It tried the King, found him guilty and had him executed on 30 January. So began the Commonwealth.

Milton fully supported the Independents' actions. Two weeks after the execution of King Charles, Milton's pamphlet *The Tenure of Kings and Magistrates* was published, 'proving that it is Lawful . . . to call to account a Tyrant, or Wicked King, and after due conviction to depose and put him to death'. Soon he was invited to be Secretary of Foreign Tongues to the Council of State of the Commonwealth of England. This Council ruled the country now, its forty-one members forming also a great majority in the House of Commons. As Milton became its first Secretary of Foreign Tongues, with the principal duty of translating into Latin any commissions from the Council to foreign powers, he was right at the heart of government. He rendered stout service to the Commonwealth beyond his duties as Secretary, writing a number of powerful tracts, pamphlets and books defending government actions. *Eikonoklastes* (breaker of an icon or image), a reply to *Eikon Basilike; the Pourtraicture of his Sacred Majestie in his Solitudes and Sufferings*, which was supposedly the work of the King himself in captivity, appeared in October 1649. Milton later wrote: 'I did not insult over fallen majesty, as is pretended; I only preferred Queen Truth to King Charles', but in fact it is also displeasingly ungenerous, even abusive in places. Shortly afterwards he was called on to refute another book, by a French professor from Leyden, Salmasius's *Defensio Regia* (*Defence of the Monarchy*). Milton published in February 1651 his *Defence of the People of England* in Latin (*Defensio pro Populo Anglicano*). It brought him European fame, but it does him little credit, being a rather tedious point-by-point refutation with a fair amount of personal abuse. It is particularly sad to think that it was by carrying out such work that he put his eyesight in danger, or made an existing weakness worse. He had lost the sight of one eye already. Milton later wrote:

> When I was publicly solicited to write a reply to the Defence of the royal cause, when I had to contend with . . . sickness, and with the apprehension of soon losing the sight of my remaining eye, and when my medical attendants clearly announced that, if I did engage in the work, it would be irreparably lost, their premonitions caused no hesitation and inspired no dismay, . . . my resolution was unshaken, though the alternative was either the loss of my sight or the desertion of my duty.

He would probably have gone on writing anyway, but it is regrettable that for so many years this great poet was fully engaged in political controversy in prose.

Shortly after he became totally blind early in 1652, his wife, to whom it appears he was completely reconciled (and who bore him four children), had another daughter and died within three days. His only son, John, died a few weeks later, aged only fifteen months. In this dreadful year in his life he seems to have shown the sort of heroic fortitude he was later to depict in the character of the hero in his drama *Samson Agonistes*. He went on at his job as Latin Secretary. In 1654 the *Defence of the People of England* was followed by the *Second Defence*, also in Latin (*Defensio Secunda*), in which he explains and defends the recent actions of Cromwell. The rule of the Council was running into difficulties. Cromwell had become Lord Protector in December 1653. Not everyone thought, as Milton thought (and expressed in the *Second Defence*) that 'Nothing in the world is more pleasing to God . . . more politically just, or more generally useful than that the worthiest man should possess sovereign power. Such, O Cromwell, all acknowledge you to be'. Opposition was building up. Cromwell's honest, effective rule was too stringent for many, and his ideas often ahead of their time. He took too little heed of what the country wanted. Before long, the country wanted Parliament back, then much of it began to want the old forms of Anglican worship back. When he tried to govern through

Parliament and it wanted its own way, just like Charles I he dissolved it. He ruled firmly and well through ten major-generals governing ten military districts, but the country stirred against military rule. Cromwell began to look more like a tyrant.

Milton had been allowed a substitute as Secretary of Foreign Tongues, because of his blindness, and instead of a salary had been given a pension for life, in 1655. In 1656 he had married again, but his second wife Katherine Woodcock had died within fifteen months and their daughter, Milton's fourth, a month later. Although relieved of routine duties, he had set about some learned projects, including a *Thesaurus* of the Latin language, a resumption of work on a *History of Britain* and a work on Christian doctrine. But public events dragged him back into polemical writing. Even in the *Second Defence*, along with praise of Cromwell there had been some expression of anxiety about dictatorship and about maintaining the separation of Church and State which Parliament had won in the Civil War. He must have viewed with misgiving Cromwell's actions. In the last year of Cromwell's life, great victories abroad in the war against Spain did not conceal his growing unpopularity in Parliament, which he dissolved again in January 1658. But the great man died in September of that year. His son briefly and ineffectually succeeded him. There followed a few confused months when the Army dissolved Parliament and abolished the Protectorate. Even at this time of great uncertainty, Milton boldly wrote in support of republicanism, attacking the monarch, and pressing for continued severance of Church from State in *The Ready and Easy Way to establish a free Commonwealth, A Treatise of Civil Power,* and *The Likeliest Means to Remove Hirelings out of the Church*, all published in 1659.

However, the country now wanted the monarchy back. Milton's fears that after the long and successful 'contestation with tyranny' the English might wish 'basely and besottedly to run their necks again into the yoke which they have broken' were realised. Charles's son was welcomed back as King Charles II in May 1660. In the months before the restoration Milton was in considerable danger, and had to go into hiding in May 1659. A recalled Parliament in the following month ordered his arrest and prosecution, and the burning of copies of his books by the public hangman, but he was quickly set at liberty. His situation was considerably reduced. From being high in government service he became a suspected and in some quarters reviled private citizen, although men like the poet Andrew Marvell (1621–78) had acted vigorously on his behalf. Probably, though, the greatest blow to him was the overthrow of all the principles which he had so actively promoted for the whole period of the Commonwealth and for some while before it. England had turned back from its glorious future – of liberty, of pure religion and decent governance – into the old monarchical days and ways. From this time, his poetry, which now became the great force of his life again, would continually be concerned with this loss and betrayal – most markedly in *Samson Agonistes* and *Paradise Lost.*

He apparently began writing *Paradise Lost* at about the time he was given a deputy in the Latin Secretaryship – 1655. (It was finished by 1665 and published in 1667.) The ambition to write a great epic poem and the idea of writing it on the great Christian subject had been in his mind for nearly twenty years. In many places we can see in this epic signs, suggestions or memories of the real-life events and issues in which Milton had been involved: conspiracy, revolt, war, betrayal, disillusionment, a leader dominated by pride and obstinacy. In some places, the poet writes briefly of himself and of his blindness. However, it is his drama *Samson Agonistes* that contains most of himself. Samson betrayed by his wife and being blinded, and despairing as he sees his people, whom he has been destined to release from enemy bondage, apparently preferring 'bondage with ease than strenuous liberty', seems to speak sometimes in the voice of the blind, disillusioned poet who had seen his hopes for a new, free, virtuous order all destroyed. Yet *Samson Agonistes* ends in triumph as well as tragedy as Samson gloriously fulfils his great destiny. One other work remained: *Paradise Regained.* It is less successful than either the epic or the drama, lacking the narrative drive, epic range and poetic splendour of the former and the dramatic power of the latter. It came late in his life, a life apparently rather miserable, despite a third marriage in 1663 when he was fifty-four. He was nearly sixty when he started *Paradise Regained* in 1667; he worked on it for over three years and published it in 1671. He died in November 1674, aged nearly sixty-six.

A note on the text

Comus was first published in 1637. 'Lycidas' appeared in a collection of elegies *Justa Edouardo King Naufrago* ('Funeral celebrations of Edward King, died in shipwreck') in 1638. A collection of Milton's poems, known as *Poems, 1645* was published on 2 January 1646. It contained the 'Nativity Ode', 'L'Allegro', 'Il Penseroso', the first and second sonnets in the selection dealt with in these Notes, and other sonnets and short pieces, including Latin poems. The other sonnets dealt with in these Notes were first published in 1673, together with some other poems.

Paradise Lost was first published in 1667 and *Samson Agonistes* in 1671. A second edition of *Paradise Lost* appeared in 1674, a few months before Milton's death. The first collection of Milton's *Poetical Works*, with a commentary on *Paradise Lost,* appeared in 1695.

Further information about the texts of individual poems is given in the introductions and in Part 5, Suggestions for further reading.

Part 2

Summaries
of SELECTED POEMS BY MILTON

'On the Morning of Christ's Nativity'

This poem was composed on Christmas Day 1629, and published in *Poems, 1645*. It consists of four introductory stanzas followed by 'The Hymn' in twenty-seven stanzas in a different metre.

The introduction simply states that this is the happy morning of the day of the month on which Jesus Christ was born, coming to the world to bring it the prospect of redemption. Christ put off the glorious brightness and majesty of his heavenly form, choosing to come to live with us as a mortal. The poet then asks the Heavenly Muse whether she cannot give a present of a poem of welcome, now, this early sunny morning. Then, seeing the Three Magi coming from the east with presents for the child Jesus, he calls on the Muse to hasten with her ode, to arrive before the Magi and to be the first to greet the Lord.

The poet begins the 'Hymn' by imagining the cold winter season in which the child of heaven was born. Nature had put off her bright aspect – for it was winter – and appeared white with snow. She had done this partly in sympathy (because Jesus had put off his godliness, assuming a man's form), partly to hide her imperfections from him. God had sent Peace to the world for the great event of the nativity, and there was no war or battle anywhere in the world.

Stanzas V and VI describe the utter peacefulness of this night, and how the winds are stilled and the stars fixed in wonder. The sun held back when day came, awed by the glory of this greater Sun.

In Stanza VIII the poet describes shepherds talking together, quite unaware that a greater shepherd had come to live on earth, until they heard divine music. Not only they, but the whole of the natural world was moved to rapture by this music, and Nature almost thought that her work, as intermediary between Heaven and Earth, was done because this wonderful music made an even greater harmony of all creation.

In Stanza XI a great light appeared to them: it was the radiance of the cherubim and seraphim praising Jesus and making wonderful music on their harps. It is said that such music had never before been made, except at the time when God was creating the world.

The poet in Stanza XIII calls on the nine spheres moving in the universe to bless human beings with their harmonious music. For, he goes on, if only we can hear this the golden age will be restored to us; Sin will die away, Hell will pass away and Truth and Justice will be restored on earth, with Mercy between them, and Heaven will be opened for us.

But the mood of exultation is checked in Stanza XVI, for Providence (good Fate) decrees that the time is not yet. The baby just born has to grow up and be crucified for us, and before the final redemption of the world there has to be the terrible blast of the trumpet sounding the summons to the Last Judgement. And then our bliss will come, which is even now beginning, with the birth of Jesus the redeemer; for Satan is beginning to realise that his power is already being limited.

And already, he goes on in Stanza XIX, the Greek oracles are silent. The local genii or nature-spirits are leaving their habitations to the sound of weeping and lament and the wood-nymphs are mourning. The Roman deities of the hearth and home and the spirits of dead ancestors are losing their power. As for the grim pagan gods (of Asia Minor) they have forsaken their temples and their worshippers, as have the animal-gods of Egypt. And as for Osiris, the chief god of the Egyptians, worshipped in the form of a bull, he is not to be seen either, but he is certainly not at rest, and his followers carry his image about in its ark in vain. He (Osiris) feels from Israel the infant Christ's influence and is blinded by the light radiating from Bethlehem. Nor can the other Egyptian gods, the crocodile god for example, withstand our Child, who even in his baby-clothes can thus show his power.

The poet continues, in Stanza XXVI, the statement of Christ's power by likening him to the sun, whose rising from his bed in the morning puts all evil spirits to flight, and fairies and elves too.

He ends, in Stanza XXVII, by calling our attention to the fact that the Virgin Mary has laid her child down to rest. It is time for him to stop. The star which led people to Bethlehem has now become a fixed star lighting the stable beneath, and that stable has become a court where angels in bright armour sit in proper ranks ready to do Christ service.

NOTES AND GLOSSARY:

Introductory stanzas:

wedded Maid and Virgin Mother: the blessed Virgin Mary was married to Joseph but still a virgin. It was important in Christian thought that she should be virginal, as she was to be the mother of the Son of God, yet she had also to be a married woman

great redemption: Christians believe that God came to earth as his Son Jesus Christ and by so doing brought assurance that he had not forgotten man, and that he would redeem mankind from the sin into which it had fallen, and in the future Second Coming of Christ would bring about the restoration of the perfection he had intended when he created the world

holy sages:	the prophets who, as recorded in the Old Testament of the Bible, foretold the coming of Christ as deliverer
unsufferable:	the light was so bright as to be unbearable
wont:	was accustomed
Trinal:	Three-fold (God the Father, the Son and the Holy Spirit)
Heavenly Muse:	Urania (*Greek*, 'the heavenly one') was in classical times the Muse of Astronomy, but Renaissance writers saw her as the Muse of Christian poetry
vein:	style

star-led wizards haste with odours sweet: the wise men (Magi) of the East who were guided to the birthplace of Christ by a new star that appeared in the sky over Bethlehem in the Judaea district of Palestine. They came (See the Bible, Matthew 2) bringing gold, frankincense and myrrh

prevent:	here, go before
angel quire:	choir of singing angels. In the Bible (Luke 2), shepherds near Bethlehem were told of the birth by 'a multitude of the heavenly host'. Milton writes of the beauty of angelic song and music in Stanzas IX–XV

secret altar touch'd with hallow'd fire: as in the Bible (Isaiah 6), it means that the Muse has received direct inspiration from God for this heavenly song

The Hymn:

while:	at the time when
rude manger:	simple, rough hay-trough (for cattle to feed from)
doff'd her gaudy trim:	taken off her gay clothing, that is, the bright colours of leaves and flowers of past seasons. This poetical 'conceit' (or exaggerated fancy) says that Nature, having put off her coloured appearance, now appears in the whiteness of new-fallen snow partly in sympathy with Christ (for God has put off divinity to appear as man) and partly to hide the sins of the world under the pure blanket of snow
wanton . . . paramour:	play amorously . . . lover
pollute:	polluted, soiled
Peace:	Peace is sent because Christ is to be the 'Prince of Peace'. Historically, also, at the time of the birth of Christ nearly two thousand years ago, there was, unusually, peace throughout the ancient world

turning sphere:	the earth was encircled by the turning spheres of the planets. See note on 'the hollow round . . .' below
harbinger:	messenger sent in advance, herald
turtle wing:	peace is seen like a winged angel; the turtle-dove is a symbol of peace; the clouds are 'amorous' because loving towards Peace
myrtle:	the tree of Venus (in Virgil's seventh eclogue) and therefore of love. Virgil (Publius Vergilius Maro) (70–19BC), the Roman poet, wrote an Epic, the *Aeneid*, and didactic poetry as well as the *Eclogues*
hooked chariot:	war-chariot with sharp hooks or blades fixed to the wheels to cut down the enemy
awful:	filled with awe
birds of calm:	kingfishers (also known as halcyons after Alcyone (wife of King Ceyx), who was turned into a kingfisher. (The Roman poet Ovid (Publius Ovidius Naso, 43BC–AD18), tells the story in *Metamorphoses* 11.) Kingfishers were believed to build their nests on the sea and hatch their young during long periods of exceptionally calm, fine weather; such weather supposedly came in the two weeks over the mid-winter period, as well as at other times
precious influence:	the stars and planets were thought to influence or have an effect upon earth and its inhabitants
And will not . . . should need:	the 'conceit' in these lines is that the sun itself delays on this morning, abashed because an even greater light has come into the world
Lucifer:	(*Latin*, bearing or bringing light) a name for the morning star, the planet Venus. There is here no suggestion of Satan; Lucifer was the name he bore as chief and brightest of the angels before his Fall
burning axle-tree:	the gleaming axle of the chariot in which the sun-god travelled the skies
mighty Pan:	the Greek god of shepherds and of pastures in mythology and pastoral poetry. In Renaissance pastoral, when shepherds could represent priests (as well as poets), Christ was thought of as Pan. In the New Testament, Christ is called 'the good shepherd', and his followers his 'flock'. In a note to 'May', in *The Shepheardes Calender* by Edmund Spenser (1552?–99), Pan 'is Christ, the very God of all shepheards, which calleth himselfe the greate and good shepherd . . . Pan signifyeth all or omnipotent, which is onely the Lord Jesus'

silly: at this time the word still meant not stupid but innocent, or simple

the hollow round/Of Cynthia's seat: the sphere of the moon. The planets, including the moon, were thought to revolve in a settled order round the earth. It was also believed that each had its own musical sound, and 'the music of the spheres' was a divine harmony of these sounds. In this lengthy passage, lines 93–147, Milton is saying that the sound of the voices and music of the angels is as beautiful as that sung by the angelic hosts while God was creating the universe (lines 118–24). It is so lovely that Nature is almost persuaded that her time of rule on earth is nearly over and that God is returning to his creation (lines 101–108)

Cherubim ... Seraphim: two of the orders of angels

unexpressive: inexpressible, that cannot be expressed (put into words)

weltering: rolling

oozy: here, simply, wet

crystal: gleaming, brilliant

And let ... blow: the organ, which can make sounds like those of all other musical instruments, itself represented harmony

ninefold harmony: the seven planets, the sphere of the fixed stars and the sphere of the *Primum Mobile* or First Mover which gave the motive force to propel all of them, make up the nine

the age of gold: the Golden Age was long ago, when war, age, death and toil were all unknown. It is a classical equivalent to the days before the Fall of Man in Christian belief

speckled: spotted (with sin)

vanity: in the Bible this often means the chief sin, that of pride

leprous: disfigured as with leprosy

Truth and Justice: they will come back to the earth and govern men's lives as they had in the Golden Age. They had fled when the Golden Age ended. Milton adds Mercy (God's and Christ's special quality for Christians), thus identifying the classical idea of the Golden Age even more closely with the Christian idea of the Second Coming of Christ to restore earth to its original heavenly state

Orb'd: encircled
tissued: 'tissue' was cloth of silk and silver, or silver and gold woven together
But wisest Fate . . . spread his throne: Milton now interrupts his vision of this happiness by reminding the reader that it is not yet time, for Christ, the baby even now innocently smiling in his cradle, has to suffer and die on the cross. Then there has to be the resurrection and in the end the Second Coming and the Judgement of the world; after which the world will return to the perfection God originally intended
ychain'd: the 'y' represents the Old English *ge-*, the prefix to the past participle. It is a Spenserian kind of archaism, occasionally used by Milton
trump of doom: the last trumpet which will sound at the Day of Judgement ('doom' = judgement). The coming of Christ in judgement may be read about in the Bible, Matthew 24
as on Mount Sinai: in the Bible, Exodus 19, God appeared out of clouds in thunder and lightning on Mount Sinai to the prophet Moses and gave him the Ten Commandments which were to be the ten rules of life for the Jews, and which came over into Christianity
the old dragon: the Devil, first so called in the Bible, Revelation 20:2 ('the dragon . . . which is the Devil')
usurped sway: he has had power (sway) over God's earth which he had usurped (wickedly taken control of)
swinges: swings, but this word also had the senses of strikes or beats, and brandishes or holds aloft in a threatening way
The oracles are dumb: the same note on 'May' in *The Shepheardes Calender* tells the story which Plutarch told 'in his booke of the ceasing of oracles', that when Christ died on the Cross, people sailing in the Mediterranean Sea heard a voice calling to the pilot to 'tel, that the great Pan was dead'. And 'at that time . . . all Oracles surceased, and enchanted spirits . . . thenceforth held theyr peace'
Apollo: the shrine of the god Apollo at Delphi was the chief centre of Greek religion. The god 'spoke' mysteriously through priests or priestesses, who were sometimes in a trance
genius: a local minor god or goddess, dwelling in or haunting springs, dales (valleys), woods, etc.

Lars ... Lemures: in Roman belief, spirits who looked after a man's house or estate; and spirits of dead ancestors who remained and had to be remembered and treated with respect and devotion. Milton shows them lamenting, because of the birth of Christ, and shows the 'flamens' (priests) in Roman temples frightened at their 'quaint' (elaborate) rites by the 'drear and dying sound'

peculiar power: particular god or spirit

Peor and Baalim: Milton now turns from the Greek and Roman divinities to the gods of the Syrians and Phoenicians. Peor was the name of a mountain and Peor-Baalim of the local deity associated with it. Baal was the Phoenician sun-god; Baalim is the plural form, standing for the many other manifestations of the sun-god

twice-battered god: Dagon, the Philistine god, (see *Samson Agonistes*) twice found face downwards (See the Bible, 1 Samuel 5) when the Philistines placed in his temple the Ark which they had captured. (The Ark was the most sacred symbol of God's presence among the Hebrews)

mooned Ashtaroth: Hebrew name (plural, meaning the goddess Ashtoreth in all her forms or manifestations) for Astarte, the supreme goddess of the Phoenicians. Her symbol and attribute was a crescent moon

Libyc Hammon: Ammon, the ram-horned Egyptian god (equivalent to Greek Zeus, Roman Jupiter), whose chief shrine was in Libya

Tyrian maids ... mourn: Tyrian, from Tyre, chief city of Phoenicia (roughly, Syria). Thammuz, the same as the Greek Adonis, in Phoenician and Syrian legend. The Greeks adopted the story of Thammuz loved and lamented over by Astarte (See the note on 'mooned Ashtaroth' above), in their tales of Adonis, loved by Aphrodite. In Phoenicia, the River Adonis turns red with mud after heavy rain in the mountains, allowing the conceit that it ran red with the blood of the wounded Thammuz/Adonis

Moloch: god of the Ammonites (a tribe in Palestine), represented in a brass, calf-headed idol inside which a fire burned

brutish gods of Nile: many of the Egyptian deities were in animal form or animal-headed

Isis; Orus; Anubis: Egyptian goddess of earth, horned like a cow; her son, the sun-god; the dog-headed or jackal-headed son of Osiris

Nor is Osiris ... worshipped ark: the chief god of the Egyptians. Memphis was the ancient capital of Egypt; Osiris was worshipped in the form of Apis, a sacred black bull in a grassy enclosure in the temple at Memphis, but now no longer since the birth of Christ. Nor can Osiris be at rest for the same reason, for like all the pagan gods he is doomed to Hell. The 'sacred chest' probably refers to the chest or casket in which an image of a god was carried by the priests

timbrelled anthems: hymns or songs sung to the accompaniment of small drums

Typhon: the Greek Typhon was a hundred-headed, serpent-tailed monster. Typhon was also the Greek name for the Egyptian crocodile god, Set. Set was the brother of Osiris, and killed him by putting him in a chest and throwing it into the River Nile. (The reference to 'chest' in line 217 may be to this chest)

orient: Eastern, where the sun rises. This stanza refers again to the dawn on Christmas morning when damned spirits of all kinds, and not only the pagan gods, troop off defeated to Hell

fetter'd ghost ... several grave: each spirit, fettered – bound or chained in fetters – to its own body, goes off to its own grave

youngest-teemed star: the newest star, that is the one that led the Magi all the way to Bethlehem to mark on the day before Christmas the stable at Bethleham where Jesus Christ was about to be born. It is now fixed in its position among the other stars

courtly stable: the humble stable has become the great court where the baby is to be honoured

Bright-harness'd angels: angels in bright armour. They wait 'in order serviceable' ready to do whatever service is required

'L'Allegro' and 'Il Penseroso'

'L'Allegro' means 'the joyful, merry, cheerful man'; 'Il Penseroso' means 'the thoughtful, pensive, contemplative man'. The two Italian words sum up the contrast these two linked poems make – between two types of man, two ways of life.

There is disagreement about when the poems were written, but it was somewhere about 1630 or 1631, and not long after Milton finished at

Cambridge. They were published in *Poems, 1645*. Some see the discussion and the contrasting as being like the sort of academic debate in Latin verse which undergraduates had to write and deliver in public as part of their academic work. Milton kept a number of these *Prolusions* that he had himself written: among them are debates 'whether day or night be the more excellent' and 'that occasional sportive exercises are not obstructive to philosophical studies'.

'L'Allegro'

The cheerful man begins by telling Melancholy to go away to some appropriately dark and dismal cell. He calls on Mirth instead to come to him, Mirth, one of the Three Graces, daughters of Venus and Bacchus – though some claim, he says, that they were born of the happy coming together of Zephyr the West Wind and Aurora goddess of the dawn. 'Hurry, nymphs,' he calls, 'and bring laughter and jollity. And also bring Liberty, and then let me be one of your company, living with you both in the free pursuit of pleasure and happiness.' He goes on to list some innocent pleasures, beginning with the pleasures of living in the country. To be up with the lark before dawn, hearing the cock crow; sometimes to hear the sounds of the hunt, sometimes going off for an early morning walk while at their work the ploughman whistles, the milkmaid sings, the mower sharpens his scythe and the shepherd counts his sheep. Then he talks of his pleasure in the landscape, of pastures and high mountains, daisy-filled meadows, little streams and broad rivers. In the landscape there are towers and battlements of some great house in which he imagines lives a beautiful lady. Near at hand, between two oaks, he envisages the smoke of a cottage chimney and two shepherds at their meal, waited on by a girl who then hastens out to help in the harvest-field – or, if it is earlier in the year than that, with haymaking. Then he thinks of church bells ringing for a holiday and the sound of fiddles to which youths and maidens dance, and, when evening comes, of the sitting round, drinking ale and hearing stories of fairies and goblins until it is time to go to bed.

The poet then turns from the pleasures of country life to those of the city: a great court tournament or a masque, perhaps, or of going to the theatre to see a clever, sophisticated play by Jonson or one of Shakespeare's sweet, natural comedies. And always, to keep off any worries or anxieties, he wants to have sweet music accompanying glorious poetry, the beauty of the human voice linked to intricate musical accompaniment. The combination as it were brings to life harmony itself, so that Orpheus, the god of music, would be wakened as he lay in heaven and would hear such music as would have persuaded Pluto, the god of the underworld, to release Orpheus's dead wife

Eurydice and allow her to rejoin him. 'Oh, Mirth, if you can give such delights, then I mean to live with you,' he concludes.

NOTES AND GLOSSARY:

Melancholy: (from *Greek*, meaning literally 'black bile') in the Middle Ages and the Renaissance period, having too much black bile in your bodily make-up was thought to cause depression of the spirits. But the 'melancholy' humour, one of the four 'humours' of the body, was associated with seriousness, intelligence, studious intellect and curiosity. Although at the beginning of 'L'Allegro' Milton relates Melancholy to things black, dark and hellish, in the companion-poem 'Il Penseroso' it is the serious, worthy, intellectual sense that is meant

Cerberus: (*Greek*) the three-headed barking monster that guards the entrance to Hades (Hell)

Stygian: of the River Styx, one of the four rivers of Hades

uncouth: unknown, unfrequented and therefore desolate

Cimmerian desert: in Homer's *Odyssey* 11 the Cimmerii live on the edge of the world, in perpetual darkness

y-clept: named

Euphrosyne: one of the Three Graces, blitheness; or, as Milton calls her, Mirth. The Three Graces represent happiness, charm and generosity. They were supposedly born at one birth to Venus and Bacchus, but Milton invents the charming idea that they were born of the west wind and the dawn ('Zephyr with Aurora')

a-maying: celebrating the coming of May, a great festival in the European Middle Ages, signalling the end of winter and the coming of summer

buxom: gracious, yielding

quips, cranks, becks: witty sayings, humorous turns of phrase, welcoming gestures

Hebe: goddess of youth, and cup-bearer to the gods

hoar: grey (from early morning mist)

cynosure: the constellation of the Lesser Bear (called by the Greeks the 'Dog's Tail') containing the Pole star, for which sailors always look when navigating as it gives the position of the north. Hence, the modern meaning of 'cynosure', looked at by all

Corydon and Thyrsis: common shepherds' names in classical and Renaissance pastoral

Phillis; Thestylis: similar, female equivalents

jocund: happy

rebecks: four-stringed fiddles

Mab... Friar's Lantern... goblin: a fairy queen (compare Mercutio's speech in William Shakespeare's (1564–1616) *Romeo and Juliet* 1.IV); a light which misleads countryfolk at night, like a 'will-o'-the-wisp'; Hobgoblin, Shakespeare's Puck or Robin Good-fellow. Fairies were mischievous but could be 'bribed' by a bowl of cream left out for them in the kitchen at night

lubber: big, ungainly

crop-full: well-fed, like a fowl whose crop is full

matins: figurative; matins is the morning church service, and the cock's crow is likened to the bell rung for the service

weeds: clothes

triumphs: pageants or fine spectacles

Rain influence: the stars 'rain' influence, letting flow a heavenly fluid which affected men's lives. The power of ladies' eyes is compared to this

judge the prize: tournaments to judge physical power, or courtly contests to judge wit or imagination, are implied

Hymen: god of marriage; he would always appear in a wedding-masque

Jonson's learned sock... Shakespeare: Ben Jonson (1572–1637), the most learned of the English dramatists of the time of Queen Elizabeth and King James I. His comedy was filled with learned comic allusions. Shakespeare's comedies by contrast are thought of as more fanciful, natural and instinctive. The 'sock' was the *soccus*, a low-heeled shoe or slipper worn by Greek and Roman comic actors. (For the buskin, worn by tragic actors, see 'Il Penseroso')

Lydian airs: the Lydian mode, one of the three modes of Greek music, thought of as rather lax and relaxing, as the next few lines show

Orpheus... Elysian... Pluto... Eurydice: Orpheus, the god of music and poetry, went to the underworld (Hades) to find his dead wife Eurydice, and so charmed Pluto, the King of Hades, with his music that she was allowed to return with him, on condition that he did not look back to see if she was following. He did look back, and lost her for ever. He is now in Elysium, the Greek abode of the fortunate dead

'Il Penseroso'

The serious or thoughtful man begins by banishing folly and superficial pleasures and calling on the goddess Melancholy to come to him. He associates peace and quiet, frugality and retirement with the goddess, welcoming all of these and especially meditation. He also asks Melancholy to whisper to Silence to come too, unless perhaps they might have the sweet, sad music of the nightingale. This thought leads him to imagine himself walking at night, looking at the moon, hearing far off the curfew bell; and then to imagine himself, if the weather is too cold for night-walking, indoors in a room lit only by the embers of the fire, the only entertainment the cricket on the hearth and the call of the night-watchman outside.

Or again, he says, let me sit up all night watching the constellations or studying the work of Plato or reading great literature. Of the latter, he mentions tragedy and epic. He wishes it were possible for Melancholy to bring to him the authors of great lost or unfinished works – including the song of Orpheus which made Pluto weep, and Chaucer's *Squire's Tale* – and he also thinks of reading the great romantic epics which carry hidden or allegorical meanings. So, he imagines, he would often spend his nights, and cloudy dawn and rainy mornings would often find him still awake. But when the sun comes out he would go to dark groves and woods where he would lie down and sleep lulled by the sound of bees and quiet-running streams, until wakened by sweet music sent by amiable spirits or by the Genius of the wood.

But he will never neglect religion and church-going, loving the dim religious light and the music of organ and choir, which seem to put him in touch with Heaven. And he imagines that in old age he will become a hermit, learning all about the stars in Heaven and the herbs and flowers of earth, and in the end understanding so much of God's handiwork, in Heaven and earth, that he will be something like a prophet of God. If Melancholy will grant him such pleasures, he concludes, he will certainly choose to live with her.

NOTES AND GLOSSARY:

bestead:	help
toys:	trifles
fond:	foolish
gaudy:	festive
Morpheus:	god of dreams. He was the son of the god of sleep
O'erlaid with black:	melancholy was caused by 'black bile' and was thought to be shown in men by a dark complexion. (This is clear in Albrecht Dürer's [1471–1528] famous engraving of *Melancolia*)

Memnon:	an Ethiopian prince, who fought for the Trojans against the Greeks, and was called the handsomest of men by Homer in the *Iliad*, his epic of the Trojan War. It may be assumed that his sister was equally beautiful
Ethiop queen that strove:	in Greek mythology, Cassiope who was 'starr'd', changed into the constellation known as Cassiopeia, as punishment for boasting that her beauty was greater than that of the Nereids. (Actually, Milton got the story slightly wrong: it was the beauty of her daughter Andromeda of which she boasted)
Vesta:	virgin, and daughter of the great god Saturn; Roman goddess of the hearth and home. Milton invents the idea that she was the mother of Melancholy, the father being her own father Saturn, the melancholy ('saturnine') god. Her throne was Mount Ida in Crete
grain:	colour or dye
cypress lawn:	the cypress tree is dark and gloomy; 'lawn' is linen. Melancholy's 'stole' (scarf or wrap) is of black linen
Forget thyself to marble:	be so lost in contemplation that you are like a marble statue
sad:	serious
Spare Fast:	eating very little food; frugality, moderation
Muses:	goddesses of learning and the arts, daughters of Zeus and Mnemosyne; there were nine
Jove:	Jupiter, the chief god of the Roman world after the overthrow of Saturn
cherub:	a member of one of the nine orders of angels
hist:	whisper to come
'Less Philomel:	unless Philomel, the nightingale
Cynthia:	the goddess of the moon, who drives a chariot pulled by dragons
curfew:	the bell rung in the Middle Ages to tell people to put out their fires. (It was not permitted to go to bed leaving the house-fire burning, for fear of fire caused by sparks on thatch and wooden dwellings, which would go unnoticed while people slept)
bellman:	the night-watchman of the Middle Ages, who sang out the time at intervals as he patrolled the sleeping streets: 'three of the clock, and all's well', for example
the Bear:	the constellation, the Great Bear

thrice-great Hermes: Hermes Trismegistus (thrice-great); name given to a legendary philosopher of the ancient world, perhaps an Egyptian god or sage, supposed to be a great teacher of occult (hidden) wisdom, of magic and mysticism

unsphere: draw down from its sphere, bring back from the other world

daemons: spirits (not necessarily 'demons', evil spirits)

sceptred: regal, because a king holds a sceptre – an ornamental rod or stick, a sign of office

Thebes: Greek city which was the scene of tragedies by the Greek writers Aeschylus (525–456BC) and Sophocles (496–405BC); it was Oedipus's city

Pelops' line: in Greek legend Pelops was the ancestor of King Agamemnon, the Greek leader in the Trojan War. He, his wife Clytemnestra and his children Orestes, Iphigenia and Electra, became the chief figures in Greek tragedies by Aeschylus and Euripides

Troy: the fall of Troy, and the fate of Trojan women, were treated in tragedies by the Greek playwright Euripides (?480–406BC)

buskin'd: Greek tragic actors wore a high-soled boot to give them greater height. (See 'L'Allegro', above, note on the comic 'sock')

Musaeus: a mythical Greek poet, pupil – perhaps son – of Orpheus

Orpheus: see 'L'Allegro', above, note

Cambuscan: Geoffrey Chaucer's (c. 1345–1400) *Squire's Tale* of a Tartar king and his three daughters was left unfinished. The lover of his daughter Canace gave her a magic ring and mirror, and gave him a horse made of brass that could carry its rider any distance in twenty-four hours

great bards beside . . . meets the ear: Milton must be thinking of Edmund Spenser here. *The Faerie Queene* (1590–6), also unfinished, was an epic romance and was allegorical (that is, more was meant than a tale of tourneys and enchantments)

trick'd: tricked out, dressed up, adorned

frounced: with curled hair

Attic boy: Eos (Greek) or Aurora (Roman), goddess of dawn, fell in love with Cephalus of Attica

minute-drops: that fall at intervals of a minute

Sylvan: Sylvanus, Roman god of woods and trees

| Genius: | in the classical world every place had its protecting local deity |
| massy proof: | of great mass, and proof against shaking or collapse |

Comus

Lines 1–92

The Attendant Spirit, introducing himself, contrasts the serene court of Jupiter, from whence he comes, with Earth, place of anxiety and effort where most people are heedless of the rewards which the virtuous will have after death. He says that his errand is to those who try to be virtuous.

He identifies the country he has come to, the island of Great Britain, and the particular part of that territory, namely the borders of Wales, home of a proud and warlike people, newly in the care of a noble lord well-fitted to govern with strength and kindness. This lord's children are on their way to the place (which in real life is Ludlow in Shropshire, castle of the Lord President of Wales, the Earl of Bridgewater, in whose honour *Comus* was written). But there is danger in this wild wood, for in it lives Comus, wild enchanter son of Bacchus, the god of wine, and of Circe, the nymph who turns men into beasts with wine from her enchanted cup. Comus is even more powerful an enchanter than his mother. Although he changes only the heads of his human victims into animal forms, not their whole bodies as Circe did, they do not understand that they have been changed and even think themselves more beautiful than before.

The Attendant Spirit says that whenever any loved by Jupiter (meaning virtuous people loved by God) come to this wood, it is his function to protect them. He then puts off his rainbow-coloured sky-robes, taking the clothes and appearance of a servant of the castle.

NOTES AND GLOSSARY:

discovers:	(*stage direction*) shows, reveals. Probably a curtain was drawn back to show the (painted) scene
Attendant Spirit:	(*stage direction)* in the surviving manuscripts 'A Guardian Spirit, or Daemon'
Jove:	Jupiter, chief of the Roman classical gods
Neptune:	God of the sea, brother of Jupiter
An old . . . arms:	the Welsh people
Bacchus:	Roman god of wine (and Milton implies criticism of wine's misuse); once, captured by Italian sailors, he charmed the ship into immobility and them into frenzy, so that the men leaped overboard and were turned into dolphins

Tyrrhene:	Tuscan
Circe:	an enchantress who could turn men into swine. Her island was Aeaea
This Nymph . . . Comus named:	Bacchus slept with Circe and the child that was conceived was Comus
Comus:	the name comes from a Greek word for revelry. He has the wine-loving nature of his father and the magic power of his mother. Comus appeared as 'The God of cheer, or the belly' in Jonson's masque *Pleasure Reconcil'd to Virtue* (1619)
Celtic and Iberian:	French and Spanish
drouth of Phoebus:	Phoebus was the Greek sun-god; so, thirst caused by the hot sun
ounce:	lynx
Iris:	goddess of the rainbow
And take . . . woods:	the part was played by Henry Lawes, the composer, and Milton pays a pretty compliment to his friend

---

Lines 93–169

He is only just in time, for Comus now noisily enters with his rioting pack of animal-headed men and women. It is now night, Comus cries, and time for drink and revelry and dance for them; strict, elderly, moral and severe people are fast asleep, but he and his companions will be like the stars, which operate at night, and like night-creatures: fairies, elves and wood-nymphs. Night, he says, is no time for sleep; there are better things to do. Venus is awake and summons to love-making. He calls on Cotytto, the wanton Thracian goddess, to hold her black chariot in which she rides with her companion Hecate, the witch-goddess of Night, until the last moment so that all nocturnal rites may be fully performed before prudish morning comes and exposes them. He calls on them to join hands and begin their round dance.

But suddenly he stops them, sensing the presence of some virtuous person. He calls on his followers to run and hide lest the approaching virgin – as his magic power tells him it is – be frightened by their number. Then he casts into the air some magic stuff which will make her see falsely. She will think him a harmless villager, and he will pretend to be friendly and courteous. He then steps aside.

NOTES AND GLOSSARY:

The star . . . fold:	this is Hesperus, the evening star
allay:	cool
steep:	deep
Rigour . . . Severity:	these are personifications; they represent rigorous, counselling, strict and severe men

Morrice:	morris dance, traditional English country-dance form: in some types, the dancers continuously shift positions
Venus:	Roman goddess of love
Cotytto:	Thracian goddess, celebrated in wanton rites held at night

Dragon womb ... Stygian ... Hecat': Stygian, of the river Styx, a river of the underworld. The underworld is briefly seen by Milton as like the inside of the dark, dreadful belly of a dragon; but there is a transfer of ideas, for Hecate, Greek underworld goddess of night and of witchcraft, drives a chariot drawn by underworld dragons

nice:	squeamish, prudish
spongy:	absorbent, like a sponge
glozing:	flattering

Lines 170–243

The lady enters, saying that she thought this was where the noise she heard came from – of riot and pleasure as of crude peasants celebrating their god Pan. She did not want to encounter such wild revellers, yet she did not know how else to get help, lost as she was in the wood. For, as she tells us, her brothers, seeing that she was tired out, left her just as evening came on to go only a little way to find berries or fruit for her. Perhaps envious Night deliberately stole them from her; why otherwise should she have made this night so dark and starless? She begins to imagine shapes and shadows and sounds calling and beckoning to her, yet though they startle, they do not terrify her, for the virtuous mind always has conscience as its companion to defend it. She says she can actually see Faith and Hope and spotless Chastity, and feels that God would send a shining protector if her life and honour were in danger. There comes a gleam of light from the shining edge of a dark cloud, and she decides that although she cannot call out loudly enough for her brothers to hear, she can at least make some sound. (Here she sings a song to Echo, asking that nymph to tell her where her brothers are.)

NOTES AND GLOSSARY:

hinds:	peasants
Pan:	Greek god of shepherds, and of hills and woods
wassailers:	revellers
votarist:	one who has taken a vow
palmer:	here, pilgrim; normally, a pilgrim who had been to the Holy Land and carried a palm-frond to prove it

Phoebus: Greek god of the sun
wain: chariot
glistering guardian: a shining guardian angel
Echo . . . Meander . . . Narcissus: Echo, a nymph whose unrequited love for Narcissus resulted in her pining away until only her voice remained. Meander is a very wandering river in Asia Minor. The nightingale's beautiful song is thought of as passionately sad, and Ovid's tale of Philomela in *Metamorphoses* explains why
Queen of parley: Echo, because she answers when spoken to
And give . . . harmonies: this last line of the song is an alexandrine, a six-stressed longer line, learned from Spenser. (The last line of a Spenserian stanza is always an alexandrine.) The extra length here suggests and emphasises the grandeur of heavenly music
resounding: is there a pun – 're-sounding' – on Echo's function here?

Lines 244–330

Comus re-enters, moved by the beauty of the song, which has given him a deep sense of sacred delight and certain bliss never felt before, even though he has often heard the singing of his mother Circe and the Sirens, so beautiful that even Scylla or Charybdis has been stilled by it. He greets her as something too wonderful to belong to this rough wood, unless indeed she is the goddess of the place; but the Lady reproaches him for such flattery.

In a brief conversation Comus learns from her that she has been separated from her two young brothers and declares that just before dark he had seen two brightly clad figures picking grapes, whom he had thought more than human. He says it would be an almost heavenly task to help her find them, and in the meantime offers her hospitality in a cottage, which she accepts. They leave the stage together and the two Brothers enter.

NOTES AND GLOSSARY:
sirens: in Homer's *Odyssey*, two maidens whose beautiful song lures sailors to shipwreck on their rocks. They are named by Milton in lines 879–80. Milton invents this idea of there being *three* sirens singing with Circe. In Homer Circe warns Odysseus against the two sirens
Naiades: fresh-water nymphs ('flowery-kirtled' suggests they are to do with earth, not sea)

Elysium:	the Greek Paradise. 'Scylla' and 'Charybdis' were respectively a rock and a whirlpool, both a danger to shipping (as were also the monsters inhabiting them), opposite one another in the straits between Italy and Sicily
Sylvan:	Sylvanus, Roman god of woods and trees
Hebe:	the young cup-bearer of the Greek gods
swink'd:	weary, from 'swink', labour

Lines 331–479

The Elder Brother calls on the stars to unmuffle and the moon to pierce the clouds. Or, if their influence is completely obscured, he asks for just a little light, even the dimmest taper from the poorest of cottages. His younger brother adds to this, pleading, if no light can be had, at least for the comfort of some sound – of flocks, or a shepherd's pipe or cock-crowing. He thinks of his poor sister, wondering first where she is and then suddenly fearing lest she may at this very moment be in the clutches of some lustful savage. The Elder Brother tells him not so anxiously to imagine the worst, and goes on to speak of their sister's virtue. She is not likely to be influenced into a bad state of mind by darkness and silence. He thinks of Virtue as having its own radiant light, and of how Wisdom will often seek out solitude in order further to contemplate Virtue.

The Second Brother agrees up to a point, but maintains that Beauty is always in extreme danger from lustful desire. As soon set out a miser's treasure by an outlaw's den and call it safe as let a helpless girl go alone through this wild place. However, the Elder Brother, while not complacent, is hopeful rather than afraid, because of their sister's 'hidden strength'. He goes on to explain that this is her chastity. No fierce savage or bandit will dare to defile her virgin purity, no evil spirit or ghost or goblin can hurt true virginity. He refers further to classical examples – Diana and Minerva – and declares that Heaven will guard any truly chaste soul, sending a thousand angels to do so. The heavenly communication with them, he continues, gradually makes the body of a chaste person take on the same chaste beauty as its soul possesses, just as lustful talk and behaviour will gradually corrupt the very soul within.

NOTES AND GLOSSARY:

Chaos: in Greek mythology, the disordered matter which existed before the creation of the world, and also the name of its ruler

Star of Arcady ... Tyrian Cynosure: pole stars used for navigation, one Greek and the other (Tyrian) Phoenician. 'Cynosure' means 'dog's tail', and the Phoenicians' polestar was in the tail of the constellation

over-exquisite: over-subtle
Hesperian Tree: Hesperus, the (Greek) evening star, presided over a paradisal island in the Western Seas. His daughters, the Hesperides, guard with a never-sleeping dragon a tree bearing golden apples there
quiver'd Nymph: this is an allusion to Spenser's Belphoebe, a 'type' of virginity, inspired by the classical Diana. (See the note on 'Dian' below)
old Schools of Greece: meaning the teaching of the Greek philosophers
Dian: Diana, Roman goddess of the moon and of hunting, and representative of virginity
Gorgon . . . Minerva: Minerva, the Roman virgin goddess of wisdom, carried a shield bearing a representation of Medusa, the snake-haired Gorgon who had the power of turning anyone who looked at her to stone
The unpolluted . . . mind: the body
Apollo: Greek god of the sun, music, poetry and learning

Lines 480–658

At this point they think they hear a cry, and stand on guard. The Attendant Spirit enters, dressed now as a shepherd. He has evidently appeared to them frequently in this guise, for the brothers recognise him and call him by name – Thyrsis. He tells them of his fears for the safety of their sister, of the sinister charms of Comus, and of the bestial revelries. He reveals that he had heard in the distance the Lady's song, and had rushed towards her, but that Comus, in disguise, had got there first. Thus thwarted, he had hastened to find the brothers.

The Elder Brother again asserts his confidence in the power of their sister's virtue, and calls to them to come with him as he sets out to confront the enchanter and free the Lady. But the Attendant Spirit tells him that his sword will be of no use, for he will be confronting magic and hellish charms. However, Thyrsis reveals to them that he has a magic root, Haemony, given him by a shepherd lad, which will protect against all enchantments. With it they may confidently attack Comus.

NOTES AND GLOSSARY:
Thyrsis: originally a shepherd (pastoral singer) in the works of the Greek pastoral poet Theocritus (c.310–250BC) and then in the Roman poet Virgil's (70–19BC) pastoral eclogues. This praise of Thyrsis, the disguise of the Attendant Spirit, for his music is a special compliment to the musician Henry Lawes who played the part and had written the music for the original performance (see also lines 84–8)

Chimeras:	monsters, part lion, dragon and goat
Acheron:	one of the rivers of Hell, here standing for Hell itself
Harpies and Hydras:	bird-like monsters with women's faces; and snake-like beasts with many heads which grew again as soon as they were cut off
Moly:	a magic herb given to Odysseus (Ulysses) to protect him from the spell of Circe in Homer
Haemony:	an invented word, perhaps suggested by an old name for Thessaly, famous for magic
Furies:	in Greek mythology winged female figures thought of as avengers of human crimes. (As the Eumenides, they dog the hero Orestes in the trilogy of plays by Aeschylus)
Vulcan:	Roman fire-god, and blacksmith of the gods

Lines 659–755

The scene changes to Comus's palace. The Lady is sitting in an enchanted chair. Comus with his followers appears and offers her his glass of magic liquor, which she brushes aside. She makes as if to get up, but Comus commands her to remain seated, saying that he has only to wave his wand to turn her to stone or to a tree. The Lady sternly replies that he cannot touch the freedom of her mind. Comus changes his manner, saying she should not be angry, and pointing out that this is a place of pleasure. He commends the cordial in his glass with its power to give great joy, and wonders why she is so cruel and unyielding to herself, for she must be tired, hungry and thirsty and the drink will restore her swiftly. She angrily refutes him, reviling him for his dishonesty in bringing her not to a safe cottage as he had offered, but to this place of grim enchantment peopled by ugly-headed monsters. Only those who are good, she concludes, can give good things.

Comus now attacks abstinence, and persuasively describes how Nature has filled the earth with fruit and flocks, and the sea with fish, and created beautiful silks for men to wear, and gold and precious stones for them. Why, he asks, should Nature have produced such bounty but for it to be used? God's generosity to man would be rebuffed if everybody abstained from rich foods, drank only water and wore only coarse woollen cloth. In any case, he goes on, if we did not make use of all these riches, Nature would be overburdened by richness and fertility, the earth overloaded, the skies black with birds. He counsels the Lady not to be deceived by Virginity; what Nature gives is meant for spending, not hoarding, and he develops the idea in relation to the Lady's great beauty, urging her suggestively to think about why she was given such beauty.

Summaries · 35

NOTES AND GLOSSARY:

Alablaster: alabaster, a fine white stone once much used for funeral statues

Daphne: Greek nymph turned into a laurel tree at her own entreaty to preserve her from the amorous god Apollo

Nepenthes . . . Helena: a pain-killing drug (literally 'grief-dispelling'); Helen of Troy (a daughter of Jupiter) was given it by a queen of Egypt after the Trojan War

budge . . . Stoic fur . . . Cynic Tub: budge is fur used to edge academic gowns, but used here it is meant scornfully of academics – perhaps with the meaning of 'pompous', for example; Stoic fur means the school of Stoicism and Cynic Tub refers to the Cynic school. Both schools of philosophy rejected pleasure, and Diogenes, a Cynic, lived in a tub in the market-place to show his contempt for wealth

---

Lines 756–900

The Lady begins her reply by saying that she had not intended to speak, but that she feels she must refute Comus's lies. Her argument is that Nature, far from intending her children to be prodigal, meant her bounty for the virtuous, who live temperately. If good men in want could have a moderate share of the excessive luxury of the rich, Nature's generosity would be fairly shared, and God more properly thanked thereby. She wonders whether to go on, wanting to say something to refute an opponent of Chastity, but declares that he would not understand if she did. Yet, she continues, if she were to try, her cause would so inspire her that the earth itself would respond in sympathy and all Comus's magic would be shaken down into fragments.

Even Comus is moved by her words, but tries to conceal the fact, sternly dismisses what he calls her 'moral babble' and tries again to make her sip the cordial. At this point the Brothers rush in, seize the glass, dash it to the ground and drive Comus and his followers out. The Attendant Spirit comes in and is dismayed to find that Comus has escaped, for without his magic wand the spell cannot be reversed and the Lady freed. But he remembers that Sabrina, the nymph of the nearby River Severn, has the power to reverse spells if properly entreated in song. Here he sings the song to Sabrina, who, attended by water-nymphs, rises singing on to the stage.

NOTES AND GLOSSARY:

Erebus: a region of Hades (*Greek*, Hell), used generally to stand for Hell

Saturn:	the Titan; one of the early Greek gods. His son Jupiter (Jove) made war against him successfully and imprisoned him in Hell
Meliboeus:	a shepherd in Virgil's pastoral eclogues, commonly used as a name for a poet in Renaissance pastoral verse. A complimentary reference to Spenser is intended: he retold the legend of Sabrina (see below) in *The Faerie Queene*
Severn . . . Sabrina:	the Severn, second river in England, which rises in Wales and flows through the Welsh border counties. The allusions are made, of course, because of the Earl of Bridgewater's position there. Sabrina was supposedly daughter of an early English king, Locrine, and granddaughter of Brutus the grandson of Aeneas (linking Britain to Virgil's *Aeneid*). Rescued from her wicked stepmother by water-nymphs she became the goddess of the river Severn
Nereus:	Greek sea-god, who lived at the bottom of the sea
Asphodil:	asphodel, a plant growing in Elysium (*Greek*, heaven) and so a symbol and agent of immortality
ambrosial:	ambrosia, food of the gods, also gives immortality
meddling Elf:	this seems to be a reference to Shakespeare's Puck in *A Midsummer Night's Dream*
Oceanus:	Greek god of water and parent of all seas, rivers, and lakes
Tethys:	wife of Oceanus
Carpathian wizard:	Proteus, a Greek sea-god, called a wizard because he could by magic change his shape, and given a hook because he was 'shepherd' of Neptune's realm
Triton:	Greek sea-god with a fish-tail; he is also Neptune's herald, and the winding shell or conch is his trumpet
Glaucus:	a Greek fisherman who became immortal as a sea-god having the gift of prophecy
Leucothea:	she and her son threw themselves into the sea to escape from her mad husband; both were turned into sea-deities
Thetis:	a daughter of Nereus, called 'silver-footed' by Homer
Parthenope, Ligea:	sirens (see note on 'sirens' above)

Lines 901–end

The Spirit implores Sabrina's help, and she goes to the Lady, sprinkling precious drops on to her and releasing her from the spell. Then she leaves, and the Lady rises from the seat while the Spirit thanks and blesses the departed Sabrina.

The Attendant Spirit calls to the Lady to leave and leads her off, guiding her to her Father's house, which is not far away, and where many of his friends are met this very night; their arrival there will double all the mirth and cheer.

The scene changes to Ludlow town and castle; there is a procession, and country dancing, and then come the Attendant Spirit with the Lady and her two Brothers, whom he presents in a sung speech to their Father and Mother, briefly reporting their triumph over sensual folly and intemperance.

The masque ends with the epilogue of the Attendant Spirit, who tells us that he is now setting off back to the skies, to the Gardens of Hesperus and the three Graces, where there is eternal summer, where young Adonis restored to life recovers from his wound, and Cupid and Psyche sojourn and are to have twin children, Youth and Joy. But the Attendant Spirit's task is over, and he leaves with a final charge to mortals to love Virtue.

NOTES AND GLOSSARY:

Amphitrite: wife of Neptune

Anchises: father of Aeneas, and so an ancestor of Sabrina (see note on 'Severn' above)

Mercury: swift-footed (he had winged heels) Roman messenger of the gods

Dryades: dryads, Greek wood-nymphs

Graces: the three goddesses (*Charites* in Greek), personification of loveliness, grace and generosity

Hours: three Greek sister-goddesses representing Spring, Summer and Winter

Adonis: beloved by the Greek goddess Aphrodite (the Roman Venus), killed by a boar but restored by the gods and allowed half the year with Aphrodite, half in the underworld. But Milton sees him not in the underworld but in Elysium for that half-year

Assyrian Queen: Aphrodite (Venus), 'on the ground' because she represents human love and 'sadly' because she has her lover for only half the year

Celestial Cupid: son of Venus; he here stands for heavenly love ('far above'), now married to the soul (Psyche)

wand'ring labours long: Psyche was separated from Cupid by the jealousy of his mother Venus, who set her many trials and tasks. (Milton mixes Latin and Greek throughout: here Eros and Aphrodite are Greek, Cupid and Venus Latin)

'Lycidas'

The poet begins by saying that he is forced to write again before he is ready. (He uses a pastoral image of unripe berries and leaves blown down before they are ready to fall in the Autumn.) The reason is that Lycidas is dead – alas, untimely – and he must pay tribute in poetry, for Lycidas was a poet too, and his dead body must not float on the sea without commemoration.

He calls on the Muses to begin (and hopes that someone may sing for him after his death), for Lycidas and he were friends from childhood.

He describes their friendship in pastoral terms, as if they had both been shepherds, looking after their flocks from dawn till night, and taking part in rural song and dance. (It is an allegory of their life at Cambridge.)

'But alas, what a terrible change now you are dead. Woods and trees and flowers all mourn your loss.

'Where were you, oh nymphs of hill and stream, when Lycidas was drowned? You cannot have been nearby, on the mountains of Denbighshire, nor on the hills of Anglesey, nor by the river Dee – but how foolish of me, for what could you have done had you been there? Even the Muse of epic poetry herself was unable to save her son, Orpheus, from that terrible death, when his severed head was cast into the river Hebrus and carried to the island of Lesbos.

'Alas, what does it avail to devote oneself to the unrewarded life of poetry and learning? Better surely to live a life of ease and pleasure. Fame, the desire for which is the last weakness of the noble-minded, is the incentive which makes a man devote himself to hard effort, rejecting pleasure. But when we hope for the reward for this dedication, suddenly death snatches us away.'

At this point Phoebus, god of poetry and of prophecy, calls to the poet: 'But Fame is not snatched away. Fame is not something to do with the mortal world, nor is it mere worldly reputation. It is God who decides and judges; you must look for and await your reward in Heaven'.

The poet returns in his thought to the world, after that sudden higher intervention from the god, and to the classical pastoral world again, invoking Theocritus's Sicilian spring, Arethusa, and Virgil's Italian river, the Mincio. We are to know that Triton has now come, on Neptune's behalf, to defend the god of the sea from any charge of responsibility for Lycidas's death. He asks the winds and waves what happened on that day, but they did not even know about the loss. And Aeolus himself, god of the winds, says that there were no winds on that day, and the sea was flat. It was the ship itself that was responsible for the loss of Lycidas.

Now came the River Cam (representing Cambridge University)

wanting to know who it was that had snatched his most precious son. And last of all – we are to imagine that there has been a procession – came St Peter, representing the universal Church. He deplores the loss of Lycidas, saying that there are many unworthy, ignorant and worldly priests in the Church whom he could have spared gladly. Their congregations are deprived of religious knowledge and instruction but, he ends, the wrath of God will fall upon them.

Again the poet, after this stern denunciation, returns to the pastoral world, calling this time, as representatives of it, on the river Alpheus in Arcadia and again on the Sicilian stream Arethusa. He asks them to summon from their valleys and all the valleys, every beautiful flower of spring and early summer, and the flower of Paradise, and daffodils, their cups filled with tears, all to be strewn over the hearse where the body of Lycidas lies. 'Or let us fancy so,' he continues, 'although we know that in fact his body is not here, but far away, washed by the seas of the world.'

The poet then adjures the mourning shepherds to weep no more, for Lycidas is not dead, although beneath the waves. Just as the sun sinks into the ocean, and rises again every day, so Lycidas sank low but now has risen to heaven through Christ's loving power, and is in the sweet society of the saints. He speaks, as it were, to Lycidas, telling him his shepherd friends no longer mourn, and tells him also that he is now the protector of all that sail in the seas where he himself was drowned.

Thus had sung the unknown – as he called himself – shepherd-poet, while the day ran on, and the shadows lengthened. And when the sun had set in the western sea, he at last stood up and adjusted his mantle, and looked onward into the future and to new interests and hopes.

NOTES AND GLOSSARY:

Lycidas: a shepherd of this name is to be found in Theocritus (*Idylls* 7) and in Virgil (*Eclogues* 9)

Laurels ... Myrtles ... Ivy: the laurel is sacred to Apollo; the myrtle to Venus; the ivy to Bacchus. These three evergreens were used singly or in combination for celebratory crowning of poets in classical times. Obviously the laurel represents reward for poetic achievement as Apollo was god of poetry. The other two are cited because both love and wine inspire a man, and also because love is one of the great subjects of poetry. The first seven lines mean that the poet is forced by Lycidas's death to take up poetry again before he is ready for it

melodious tear: tearful melody; the Latin word *lacrimae* (tears) was also used as a title for a collection of elegiac verse and applied to elegies

Sisters . . . well: the nine Muses, goddesses of learning and the arts, whose holy place was a spring – the Pierian Spring – at the foot of Mount Olympus, which was the 'throne' of Jupiter and the other gods

Muse: here, simply a poet, one inspired by the Muse

For we . . . song: Milton follows the pastoral conventions in presenting King and himself as shepherds. This account is really an allegorical representation of their days at Cambridge University. Shepherd life represents writing poetry and learning. The dance and song probably refer to pastimes. 'Old Damoetas' is perhaps a college tutor who approved of their work

gray-fly: some kind of flying beetle or other insect that makes a noise when flying

sultry: this suggests the hot middle of the day

mourn: this is the 'poetic fallacy': human emotions attributed to trees, flowers and other natural objects

taint-worm . . . weanling: a disease in sheep and cattle; newly weaned, that is no longer dependent on the mother's milk

wardrop: wardrobe, clothes. This reference is to late frost that sometimes kills the early spring flowers

For neither . . . stream: King was drowned off the coast of North Wales near the island of Anglesey. These references are to hills and mountains of Denbighshire and the island of Anglesey, and to the River Dee which enters the sea nearby. Druids were a Celtic (Welsh) order of priests

The Muse: Calliope, Muse of Epic poetry, was the mother of Orpheus, great classical symbol of 'the poet'. But even she was unable to protect him from the drunken Thracian Maenads, who tore him to pieces and threw his head into the River Hebrus in Thrace, whence it was carried on to the island of Lesbos

shepherd's trade . . meditate the thankless Muse: both phrases mean the profession of poetry

Amaryllis . . . Neaera's hair: both names are common in pastoral poetry for maidens loved by shepherds. There are also references in pastoral poetry to Neaera's tangled hair, beginning with the Roman poet Tibullus (*c.*54–19BC)

blind Fury: actually, it was one of the Three Fates, not Furies, whose job it was to cut the thread of life which had been spun and measured by the other two. But the idea of a blind Fury is even more powerful

Phoebus replied: the god of poetry seems to call down to the poet, refuting his thoughts about the lack of reward for a life of dedication to study and poetry. Phoebus says that the reward can be everlasting Fame. The fame he means is not something that grows on earth; nor is it like the thin gold or silver leaf placed under a jewel to give it the appearance of greater brilliance; nor is it merely notoriety. It is what is adjudged by Jove (Milton of course means God) to be virtuous and of real worth in His eyes

fountain Arethuse: the source of the river of that name in Sicily

Mincius: a river in North Italy. Virgil was born at Mantua – built on two islands in the river Mincio – and describes its sedges and reeds and its slow windings in the *Georgics* 3, and also refers to it in *Eclogues* 7 and in *Aeneid* 10

Because Sicily was the original home of pastoral, Theocritus having been born there, and because of Virgil's pastoral writing in the works just mentioned, all references to Sicily or any place or river in Sicily, and to Virgil or to rural places in Italy mentioned by him, are meant to convey automatically the idea of 'pastoral'

herald of the sea: See note to 'Triton' in *Comus*, above

Neptune: chief god of the sea

felon: in Milton's time this could mean either wicked or wild, savage. Either is, indeed both are, appropriate here

rugged: rough, stormy

Hippotades: 'son of Hippotes'. This was Aeolus, god of winds

Panope: a Nereid, or sea-nymph

Built in the eclipse: an eclipse of the sun or moon (when either is partially or totally obscured from earth) was taken as a sign of ill-omen. So this means 'ill-omened ship'

Camus: stands for the River Cam which runs through and gives its name to Cambridge. His 'mantle hairy' and 'bonnet sedge' are appropriate as costume for the river-god of the University city, suggesting bordering woods and the sedge and reeds at the water's edge

like to that sanguine flower: the hyacinth, named after Hyacinthus, a youth loved by the god of poetry, Apollo, who killed him accidentally while they were playing at quoits. Apollo, making the flower spring from Hyacinth's blood, marked the Greek for 'Alas' (AI)

42 · Summaries

on its leaves, as Ovid tells in *Metamorphoses* 10, and
the early Greek pastoral writer Theocritus refers to
it twice in *Idylls* 10 and *Lament for Bion*. The flower
is 'sanguine' because of Hyacinth's blood: the Latin
for 'blood' is *sanguis*

pilot of the Galilean lake: St Peter was a fisherman on the Sea of Galilee
(See the Bible, Luke 5)

keys: St Peter's sign in art and heraldry is two crossed
keys, because Christ gave him the keys which open
the way to salvation (See the Bible, Matthew 16).
There are two keys, one of which opens the way for
the virtuous and the other shuts out the wicked

How well . . . no more: St Peter, Bishop of Rome, founder of the
Christian Church, here attacks corruption and
inadequacy in the Church. The 'pastoral' image
('pastor' as shepherd) is continued. Shepherds are
here priests, the flock their people or congregation.
The ones who have crept into the fold 'for their
bellies' sake', and have 'scrambled' to be at the
shearer's feast, are bad priests who are unworthy of
their priesthood, but have managed to get themselves into the Church for what they can get out of it
to their own advantage. They are ignorant and
incapable (hardly able to use a sheep-hook).

Milton then slips into seeing these bad shepherds
as bad poets, too, whose songs are 'lean and flashy'.
He goes back to the other pastoral image, shepherd
as priest, in the passage (125–9) describing how the
congregations look up for spiritual teaching and
food, but are not fed by their ignorant priests, and
so their bellies swell with wind, and they fall prey to
disease. Apart from these losses, they are daily
devoured by wolves. The wolves represent the
Church of Rome because the Catholics are able to
make many converts on account of the inadequacy
of the Anglican (Church of England) priests St Peter
(and Milton) is attacking. But, he ends, the two-
handed sword of retribution (or, if you like, of
God's justice) is waiting for them and will strike
them dead.

Alpheus: a river, which was in love with Arethusa, nymph of
the river of that name in Sicily. This connects it with
pastoral, the first great pastoral poet being
Theocritus, a Sicilian of Greek descent

swart star:	the 'dog star', Sirius, is associated with hot weather and is called 'swart', meaning swarthy, sun-burned, by association
quaint enamelled:	curiously decorated and brightly coloured (like enamel-work)
rathe:	early; a dialect word used by Spenser in the *Calender* (July and September)
forsaken dies:	in *The Winter's Tale* (IV.3.122) Shakespeare tells of primroses 'that die unmarried'
freaked:	a word coined by Milton. Probably 'streaked' with black ('jet')
laureate:	covered with laurels, representing poetic achievement (see note on 'laurels', above)
Hebrides:	islands off the north-west coast of Scotland
whelming:	over-whelming, overcoming
our moist vows denied:	even though we pray sorrowfully (with tears), we are refused the sight of Lycidas's body
fable of Bellerus old:	Bellerium is a Latin name for the south-western tip of England known as Land's End. Milton has invented a fabulous Bellerus for the area: 'fable of Bellerus old' means 'where the story of old Bellerus is said to have taken place'
guarded mount ... Namancos ... Bayona:	St Michael's Mount near Land's End in south Cornwall, which becomes an island at high tide. (There is one across the English Channel off the coast of France too.) The Archangel Michael was said to have appeared to monks in the monastery there. Namancos and Bayona are on the north coast of Spain, thought of as looking towards England. St Michael is thought of as being on the watch to warn England of danger from Catholic Spain.
	The elegist is wondering whether the body of Lycidas has been washed under the sea from where King was drowned in North Wales either north to the west of Scotland or south to Cornwall or even the coast of Spain
dolphin:	there was a classical figure, Arion, a writer of song and poetry, who was rescued from the sea and carried on his back by a dolphin which had been pleased by his song
Weep no more ... perilous flood:	Renaissance pastoral elegy often changed from sad lament to happiness and triumph, as 'Lycidas' does

day-star: the sun
tricks: dresses or brightens
new spangled ore: new, dazzling gold
that walked the waves: Christ, who walked on the sea (Matthew 14).
Because of God's power, the virtuous Lycidas has
gone up to Heaven
nectar: in *Paradise Lost* 4.240 Milton tells that the streams
in Eden run with nectar, the drink of the classical
gods
oozy: wet (from the sea)
unexpressive: that cannot be expressed, inexpressible, beyond the
power of human expression
nuptial song: marriage song, for the 'marriage of the Lamb' – the
symbolic marriage of Christ to his church, that is,
his faithful people, as foretold in the Bible,
Revelation 19:7
for ever from his eyes: a deliberate echo of 'God shall wipe away all tears
from their eyes' (Revelation 7:17). (The Book of the
Revelation of St John, the last book in the Bible,
deals with prophecy of the future victory of Christ
over the wickedness of the fallen world)
Genius: to the Greeks or Romans a local deity (god) who
looked after that place or area. (See 'On the
Morning of Christ's Nativity', lines 181–8). Lycidas
is to be protector of those who travel in the
dangerous seas off the coast of Anglesey and North
Wales
Thus sang . . . : Notice that the poet, who has written so far in the
first person ('I') now changes to the third person
('he'), and so steps back, as it were, and makes the
reader step back and detach himself from grief
uncouth: unknown, but with a possible further mock-modest
suggestion of unskilful
Doric lay: the early pastoral poets, Theocritus, Bion and
Moschus, all wrote in the Doric dialect of Greek.
Syracuse in Sicily where they came from was a
Dorian colony

Some sonnets

Introduction: the sonnet

The sonnet, originally an Italian form, came to England in the sixteenth century, the first English sonneteer probably being Sir Thomas Wyatt (1503–42). The Italian sonnet, established and perfected by Petrarch (1304–74), was predominantly but not exclusively used for serious love-poetry. It consisted of fourteen lines, divided into the octave (eight lines) and the sestet (six lines). The rhyme-scheme was usually *abba abba* in the octave, *cde cde* in the sestet, though the latter may vary, and contain only two rhymes. (The English sonnet developed into three quatrains [four-line units] and a concluding couplet rhyming *abab cdcd efef gg*; it is often called the Shakespearean sonnet.)

The Italian or Petrarchan sonnet is excellent for a statement, or presentation of an idea, situation or incident in the octave, which is modified, developed or resolved in the sestet. The English form obviously has a different emphasis and balance, with twelve lines, in which the statement is presented, instead of eight, and a concluding couplet for a swift, decisive and often ironic or comic climax or conclusion.

Milton uses the Italian form, which by his time had developed, in the hands of Petrarch's successors, so that it seemed more like Latin classical verse, more Virgilian or Horatian. Milton's tendency towards the longer verse-paragraph (as seen in 'L'Allegro', 'Il Penseroso' and 'Lycidas', not to mention the epic and dramatic poems) is also apparent in his sonnets. They do not have the clear separation of octave and sestet of the Italian sonnet, nor the sense of stanzas within the poem. The long stride of Milton is usually there, and appropriately, for he used the sonnet (which had almost died out by his time) not for love-poetry or light charming playfulness but for presenting much more serious subjects, weighty contemporary topics, the praise of great men and condemnation of others, and also for the expression of deep personal feeling. They are the most serious sonnets in English up to that time (yet he is also capable of lightness of touch and even humour).

[On his being arrived to the age of twenty-four]

Milton became twenty-four on 9 December 1631, and this poem was presumably written at about that time.

Milton is regretful that, although he is now twenty-four, in the 'late spring' of his life, there has been no spring-like 'flowering' of poetry from him. He looks younger than he is, and indeed he is more immature than others of his age. Yet he will not swerve from his resolve to dedicate his life to God's service and to living in obedience to His will, whether that means a great or just a commonplace or ordinary career.

The final couplet means: 'All my life, if only I am given grace so to live, will be passed always as if God were watching me; that is, with virtuous dedication to God's will.

NOTES AND GLOSSARY:

career: speed
no bud or blossom shew'th: he means he has not yet written any poetry
semblance: appearance
more timely-happy: maturing earlier
still: always
lot: destiny
task-master: God

'When the Assault was Intended to the City'

Written probably in November 1642, two months or so after the Civil War broke out, the sonnet is addressed to any officer of the Royalist forces invading London who may come to Milton's house with violent intentions. When the war broke out in August 1642, the Royalists advanced swiftly towards London, defeating a Parliamentary force at Brentford just to the west. Milton, whose wife Mary Powell had left him to return to her (Royalist) parents, was living in Aldersgate Street. He calls on the supposed enemy officer to spare his house, because it is the house of a poet, as Alexander the Great spared the house of Pindar, and as the Spartans and their allies spared the city of Athens because it was the home of Euripides. A poet, Milton says, can reward such an act of mercy with poetic fame and undying praise (and this poem is, as it were, 'payment in advance').

NOTES AND GLOSSARY:

colonel: here, pronounced as three-syllabled
whose chance: who by chance
charms: both 'songs' and 'spells'
muses' bower: where the muses live – meaning where poets and poetry reside
Emathian: Alexander the Great of Macedonia (356–323BC). He sacked the city of Thebes in 335BC, sparing only the house of the Greek poet Pindar (c.522–440BC)
repeated air ... : when Lysander in 404BC had captured Athens and it was proposed to destroy the city, a man was heard singing the first chorus from Euripides's play *Electra* which so moved the conquerors that they decided to spare the city

'To Mr H. Lawes on his Airs'

Henry Lawes (1596–1662) was a leading musician of his time. He was an official of the Chapel Royal, one of the King's Musicians. He was connected with the household of the Earl of Bridgewater, as music-tutor. In 1634, Milton was asked by Lawes to write something to celebrate the taking-up of office by the Earl of Bridgewater as President of the Council of Wales. The long masque *Comus*, with music by Lawes, was the result. This sonnet, dated 9 February 1646, an affectionate tribute to a friend, especially praises Lawes for respecting and fully bringing out in his 'airs' the meaning of the poetry. Because he thus honours poetry, he shall himself be honoured, and the poet Dante shall set him higher in the after-life even than his own friend Casella. Lawes's first of three volumes of *Airs and Dialogues* appeared in 1653.

NOTES AND GLOSSARY:

Airs:	simple tunes, either sung or played on musical instruments
well-measured:	skilfully rhythmic
span:	join, link
scan:	count syllables in verse
Midas' ears:	in Greek mythology, Midas, a King of Phrygia, whose ears were turned into ass's ears by Apollo as a punishment for preferring, in a music-contest, the music of Pan to that of Apollo. The story is told in Ovid's *Metamorphoses* 11
committing:	here, opposing
Envy to look wan:	Envy, always depicted as pale (compare 'pale with envy'), will look even paler
writ:	written about as, remembered or recorded as
humour:	fit, suit
lend her wing:	help with her inspiration
To honour . . . or story:	'To do honour to you, the chief of the followers of Phoebus [seen as god of music here], who sets their best lines of poetry or their best stories to music'
Dante:	the great Italian poet (1265–1321) of the Renaissance, the first great poet to write not in Latin only but his own language: indeed, he founded, in a sense, the modern language, for his Tuscan became Italian
Casella:	in his *Purgatorio* 2 he tells of his imagined meeting with the ghost of Casella, a Florentine musician, among a crowd of souls just arrived in Purgatory, and of how he asked him to sing. Casella sang a *canzone* of Dante's

Purgatory: where the souls of those who have died in a state of grace undergo a limited amount of suffering to expiate their (not very grave) sins and become purified; 'milder' may mean that the entrance or threshold to Purgatory is milder than other parts of it, or that Purgatory is milder (less dreadful) than Hell

'On the Detraction which followed upon my Writing Certain Treatises' (?1647)

Milton was much attacked, after his marriage and his wife's hasty desertion of him, for writing pamphlets proposing that divorce should be possible not only for adultery but for people who really could not live happily together. The first was *The Doctrine and Discipline of Divorce* (1643). The fourth was *Tetrachordon* (1645). Notes on this amusing sonnet are included because of its colloquial and conversational tone, although it is a narrow and not very important poem. It was probably written in 1647, after his wife had returned to him, and he presumably no longer had a personal interest in the matter. In it Milton launches an attack on those who have ignored his treatise *Tetrachordon*, being frightened off by its title – but why, he asks, should people be put off by a word like that when all these rough Scotch names are now so familiar that we can all pronounce them. In a way, the sonnet attacks the Scots, who were now prominent in England, and whose form of religion, Presbyterianism, had now become the established religion – not to Milton's pleasure. It was also the Presbyterian influence which threatened toleration not only in religion but in publishing and Milton defied it by publishing his tracts without a licence.

NOTES AND GLOSSARY:

Tetrachordon: (*Greek*) four-stringed. On the title-page Milton explains that it refers to 'the four chief places in Scripture, which treat of Marriage, or nullities in Marriage' in the Bible, in Genesis, Deuteronomy, Matthew and Corinthians

numbering: counting among its readers

stall-reader: someone reading at a bookseller's stall (an open-air stand, rather than a shop, from which things are sold)

in file: in a row

spelling false: spelling out or interpreting wrongly

Mile-End Green: the farthest suburb, on the eastern edge of London, in Milton's time

Gordon, Colkitto ... Macdonnel ... Galasp [Gillespie]: Scottish names, which sound 'rugged' or rough to English ears. The long struggle in England between King Charles I and Parliament had been brought to a point by Scottish anger, leading to a brief invasion of northern England in 1639, because of the King's attempt to force them in religious matters. He tried to replace their Presbyterian form of religion – a more democratic form with ministers (priests or clergy) elected and paid for by the congregations, without any hierarchy of bishops and other high officers of the Church – by a return to the Anglican form

Those ... sleek: 'Those rough names are getting easy for us to speak – as if they were as smooth ('sleek') – as our own'

Quintilian: (AD35–*c*.95) a classical authority on style, who in his discussion of 'barbarisms' includes the use of foreign words

Sir John Cheek: Cheke (1514–57) was first Professor of Greek at Cambridge and tutor to the young King Edward VI

Hated not ... asp: 'did not hate learning more than they hated toads or snakes'

'On The Lord General Fairfax at the siege of Colchester'

Sir Thomas Fairfax (1612–71) was a leading military figure on the Parliament side in the English Civil Wars (August 1641–August 1646 and April–August 1648). He was – with Cromwell – the most successful Parliamentarian general, and became Commander-in-Chief of the New Model Army in January 1645. In that year he added to the impressive list of his victories Naseby, Leicester, Langport, Bridgewater and Bristol, and in the following year Torrington (Devon), Exeter and Oxford. It could almost be said that the victory over the King depended on the brilliance of the generalship of these two men, Fairfax and Cromwell.

The poem, although not published in Milton's lifetime, indeed not until 1694, was written in August 1648.

NOTES AND GLOSSARY:

name in arms: fame as a soldier in war

virtue: courage, valour

Hydra heads: in classical mythology the Hydra was a snake-like monster with nine (or more) heads, which, if cut off, grew again. The rebellions are described as hydra-headed because they break out in numerous places. Milton is referring to the Second Civil War, actually more a series of separate but planned Royalist outbreaks in different parts of the country together with a Scottish invasion. It ended after Cromwell had defeated the Royalists with his Parliamentary army in South Wales and had then moved to defeat the Scottish invaders, and Fairfax had quelled actions in Kent and then in Essex, where he successfully besieged and captured Colchester

the false North ... broken league: false because the Scots had been allied with Parliament since 1643 (by the Solemn League and Covenant) but now (1648) the Scottish Army came into England to support the Royalists, having broken the 'League' (alliance or association)

imp their serpent wings: 'serpent' conveys the meaning of 'deceitful'; 'imp' is a term from hawking; when a falcon had broken wing-feathers, spoiling its power of flight, new feathers would be 'imped' (fixed to the stumps)

a nobler task: Milton means that he hopes Fairfax, after his success in war, will now lead the country in peace. (But it was not to be: Fairfax would not support those wanting the King to be executed, and gradually withdrew into private life)

public faith ... land: Milton condemns the 'fraud' (financial deceit and dishonesty), 'avarice' (greed) and 'rapine' (plunder or extortion and robbery) that had followed the end of the First Civil War and the victory of the Presbyterian-dominated Parliament

---

'To the Lord General Cromwell, May 1652, on the proposals of certain ministers at the Committee for Propagation of the Gospel'

This committee, of which Cromwell was a member, had been set up in February 1652 to consider religious matters. Some members of the committee wanted to set up an Established Church with ministers paid by the state, and some limitation on freedom of worship outside it. Milton is strongly opposed to any constraint on complete freedom and to intolerance, as Cromwell was also known to be. In this sonnet, Milton frankly and manfully praises 'our chief of men' and goes on to urge him to achieve victories in peace as great as his victories in war by saving the principle of freedom of belief and worship, and opposing the idea of 'mercenary' priests paid by the state – and therefore 'hired', and by implication concerned less with principle than with payment.

NOTES AND GLOSSARY:

crowned Fortune ... God's trophies: Milton says that the successful servant of God (Cromwell) has overcome the proud pagan goddess Fortune (Destiny). But there is reference too to Cromwell's victories over King Charles I, and also over his son whom he defeated at Worcester in 1651 after the latter had been crowned King in Scotland. Some see a reference to the beheading of Charles I in the reference to 'neck'

reared: raised up

trophies: weapons and other spoils of war heaped up as a monument to victory

Darwen: a small stream joining the River Ribble near Preston in Lancashire, where Cromwell defeated the Scottish invasion in August 1648

imbrued: stained

Dunbar: in Berwickshire, where Cromwell routed another Scottish army in September 1650

Worcester's laureate wreath: Cromwell's crowning victory at Worcester in September 1651 (a Roman victor was crowned with a wreath of laurel leaves) was over the Royalist Scottish army led by the beheaded King's son, who was to become Charles II in 1660

secular chains: controls imposed by the civil power of the state: Milton does not want religion to be controlled by the state

hireling: mercenary, doing things for money

maw: literally, mouth; but here, by implication, belly, meaning greed

---

[On his blindness]

Milton began to suffer from failing sight in 1644, and lost the sight of his left eye by 1650. It is not known for certain when this sonnet was written, but it seems to have been sometime between February 1652 and 1655.

NOTES AND GLOSSARY:

spent: extinguished

Ere: before

half my days: Milton was forty-three in 1652. He was well past half the allotted span (three-score years and ten: seventy years) but his father had lived to at least eighty-four and apparently had been still able to read without spectacles talent: the modern word, meaning skill, or special ability, derives from a word which meant a particular measure of money. In the Parable of the Talents (See the Bible, Matthew 25), one servant receives one talent of money in trust from his lord, buries it and thus gets no increase or profit from it. His fellows, who invested or traded with their talents, doubled the value. The servant who hid his talent is punished by having it taken back. Milton is alluding to this story, with reference to his special ability – and serious vocation – as a poet, which he thinks will be impossible for him now he is blind. (In fact, the great epic poem *Paradise Lost*, which he dictated, being unable to see to write, and other works, were written after he became blind)

lodged with me: entrusted, given into my care

bent: inclined to, therefore eager to

fondly: foolishly

prevent: forestall, come before or anticipate

murmur: here, of complaint or grievance

thousands: that is, of angels; 'angel' is from the Greek word meaning 'messenger'

post: travel fast; in this way the angels carry messages from God to earth

They ... wait: in this famous line Milton contrasts the speeding angel-messengers of lines 12 and 13 with those virtuous souls – and he clearly includes himself – who serve God on earth and await his word and decisions. It suggests that Milton is thinking of standing and waiting as less significant even if equally virtuous service

---

[To Cyriack Skinner, on his blindness]

Skinner was a friend and was probably a pupil when Milton took in pupils in about 1640. This sonnet presents a rather different attitude to his blindness from the preceding one, and it was certainly written quite a long time later. The first line says that it is three years since he could see; the earlier sonnet probably dates from 1652 and this from 1655.

Milton is certainly reconciled to his misfortune. He does not complain or 'murmur', but with heroic acceptance declares that he will not give up hope or determination. He ends by declaring that what keeps up his spirits is the knowledge that he has lost his sight in a good cause, that of Liberty. He also looks forward to further activity. In 1655 his salary was replaced by a pension for life and he was probably in this sonnet writing hopefully of future literary projects.

Notice the clear, simple, unadorned English of this sonnet, and the open, man-to-man tone of address.

NOTES AND GLOSSARY:

Against Heaven's hand or will: against what God has done or decides
bate a jot: lessen in even the smallest way
bear up and steer: a metaphor from sailing. To bear up is to bring the boat into the wind
conscience: consciousness
overplied: overworked
mask: masque, pageant

'On the late Massacre in Piemont'

The Vaudois or Valdenses were members of a sect founded in the twelfth century by the Frenchman Peter Valdes of Lyons. They practised simple Christianity and the virtues of poverty and self-denial. They were excommunicated (expelled) by the Roman Catholic Church in 1215. They were living in the seventeenth century in some Alpine valleys on the borders of France and Italy, where the remoteness, especially from any powerful church authority, and a treaty with the Duke of Savoy in 1561 which granted them toleration, protected them. Suddenly, in 1655, the army of the Duke of that time attacked them, massacring many and laying waste their villages, and hanging those whom they caught trying to escape. Cromwell, now in the supreme position as Lord Protector, saw himself and England as champions of Protestantism in Europe. He protested sharply about the massacre and set about organising protest throughout Europe, including the use of force if necessary. Milton, who was still Secretary 'for Foreign Tongues', wrote many of the letters of protest.

In this sonnet, thought to date from about May 1655, he calls on God to avenge the massacred Valdenses, whose purity of religion must not be forgotten. They were real worshippers of God, slain by the Piedmontese, their bodies flung over cliffs. May their martyrdom eventually influence the Catholic world, so that Catholics will leave that religion which is doomed, like Babylon of old, to destruction.

NOTES AND GLOSSARY:

saints: the Valdenses are called this not only because of their virtuous and religious life, but also because the Puritans called all true believers saints
stocks and stones: images of wood and of stone. A slighting reference to Catholic worship of images

fold:	sheep-fold, enclosure in which sheep were kept for their safety
Piemontese:	Italian spelling for Piedmontese, from the Piedmont district of Savoy, partly Italian, partly French. The word means 'mountain-foot', or foothills (here, below the Alps)
that rolled . . . rocks:	Some of the Valdenses were hunted over cliffs or precipices by the Piedmontese
redoubled:	echoed
sway:	rule or reign
triple Tyrant:	the Pope, whose crown is three-tiered
Babylonian:	Rome was often identified in the Renaissance, especially by Protestants, with Babylon, the wicked and powerful city in ancient Mesopotamia, the destruction of which is foretold in the Bible, in Revelation

---

[On His Deceased Wife]

Which wife – Milton had three – was the 'late espoused saint'? His first wife, to whom he was certainly at first unhappily married, died in 1652. 'Late espoused', meaning recently married, would seem to fit his second wife better. He married her in November 1656 and she died on 3 February 1658. As the poem was probably written in 1658, she looks more likely, yet the reference in line five to 'childbed taint' fits the first wife better. She had died before the end of the period of purification after childbirth. Yet again, the name of the second wife, Katharine, is derived from the Greek word for 'pure', and the stress on purity and purification suggests that Katharine Woodcock, not Mary Powell the first wife, is meant. On the whole, Katharine, the second wife, is the stronger candidate.

NOTES AND GLOSSARY:

saint:	good 'saintly' woman, with also a suggestion of a virtuous soul in Heaven
Alcestis:	in the play *Alcestis* by the Greek dramatist Euripides (*c.*480–406BC) she gives her life for her husband but is brought back from the underworld to her husband Admetus by Hercules, 'Jove's great son'
old law:	old Jewish law laid down that a woman after childbirth is 'unclean' for a period of about eighty days, following which she has to undergo a 'purification' ceremony

without restraint:	without anything to hinder or prevent it. He means that he will have 'full sight' of her in Heaven, being no longer blind
fancied sight:	he imagined that he could see
inclined:	bent forward

Samson Agonistes

Lines 1–114 Prologos

The blind Samson in prison at Gaza asks to be led to the bank where he normally sits when not forced to work, to enjoy the fresh air. He has a sort of 'holiday' today for it is the Philistine feast for their god Dagon. If his body can rest, his mind cannot, thronging as it is with bitter thoughts. He wonders about the prophecy that he was destined for great deeds now he is a blinded, betrayed prisoner; and why his great strength, intended to be employed in the freeing of the Israelites from the Philistines, is only used in prison-slavery. But he checks, and reviles himself for his folly in having revealed the secret of his great strength (which was in his hair) to a woman. If only his mind had been as strong as his body. He bewails his miseries, chief of which is his blindness, which makes him inferior to the lowest creeping thing. He hears people approaching.

NOTES AND GLOSSARY:

Agonistes: this word has several significances: contestant, champion, one who struggles

Lines 115–75 Parode: the first speech of the Chorus

It is a group of men of Dan, his own tribe. They form the Chorus (or group of people who appear in Greek tragedy to interpret and comment on the action). They are dismayed at the sight of Samson, whom they now recall in the days of his strength slaying a thousand with the jaw-bone of an ass and bearing away on his shoulders the gates of Gaza. They do not know which to bewail first, his being imprisoned or his having been blinded, and feel that he is doubly imprisoned, the worse being the prison of his own thoughts. It presents to them a terrible moral, about the uncertainty of human life, that the strongest of men from the highest should have been brought to the lowest pitch. Samson's strength, if associated with virtue, might have conquered the earth.

NOTES AND GLOSSARY:

Chalybean: of the Chalybes, a tribe of famous metal-workers from Scythia in Asia Minor

Adamantean proof:	adamant: originally, hard steel; later, diamond
Ascalonite:	belonging to Askelon, one of the five chief Philistine cities
fore-skins:	standing for the Philistines, who, unlike the Jewish peoples, did not circumcise their boy-children
Azza:	Gaza
Hebron:	thirty miles east of Gaza. By Mosaic law, a Sabbath's journey must not be as much as a mile
to bear up Heav'n:	Samson in this exploit was like the great Titan in Greek mythology, Atlas, condemned by Zeus to support the sky on his head and hands

---

Lines 176–292 The first Episode: Samson and the Chorus

Samson becomes aware of them and they greet him solicitously. He welcomes them as true friends, again bitterly reproaches himself, assuming that he is mocked and scorned for his folly. If only, he says again, he had as much wisdom as strength. They say that the wisest can make mistakes, and go on to wonder why he had ever married a Philistine woman, rather than one of his own tribe. Samson says that he first chose a Philistine, despite the opposition of his parents because she was not Jewish, because she pleased him and he thought God intended it as part of his plan for the deliverance of the Israelites. But she proved false, and he married Dalila, another Philistine, for the same reasons. The Chorus acknowledges that Samson was always eager in the cause of his people, but points out that the Israelites are still in bondage. Samson says he blames their leaders, who ignored his great military deeds, and who later, to placate the enemy, gave him into their hands. However, he had easily broken the cords with which they had bound him, had seized the jaw-bone of an ass and routed the enemy host. If only the men of Judah had supported him, they could have captured Gath (a major Philistine city.) But, he goes on, when nations get corrupt they slackly accept bondage rather than face fighting for freedom, and envy, suspect and even desert those who seek to free them.

NOTES AND GLOSSARY:

thy friends:	the Chorus is composed of men from Samson's own district and tribe (the tribe of Dan) in the valley west of Jerusalem; Zora was his birthplace
Timna:	Timnath, a Philistine city. Samson first wanted to marry a Philistine girl from Timnath. Jews were forbidden to marry 'infidels', that is, Gentiles or non-Jews, but Samson says his wish was approved by God as part of his plan to begin the deliverance of the Israelites from the Philistine oppression

false: she gave away the secret riddle and then married his groomsman or 'best man'

Dalila: must be accented on the first syllable: Dálila

But they persisted . . . they serve: told in the Bible, Judges 15. Samson routed the Philistines and retired to Etam in Judah. The Philistines with more forces came to seek him, and the men of Judah, instead of rallying to Samson, in order not to anger the enemy bound him and surrendered him to them. Probably Milton means the reader to think of the English who, after Cromwell had succeeded in 1649 in the Civil War in destroying the monarchy, gradually turned and welcomed the King back in 1660

Thy words . . . Shibboleth: other examples from the Bible (Judges 8, 11 and 12) of people failing to support or be loyal to their heroic leaders or deliverers

Shibboleth: the ability to pronounce the word (meaning either 'ear of corn' or 'river in flood') was used as a test of tribal identity (Judges 12)

Lines 293–325 The first Stasimon (Song) of the Chorus

The Chorus recalls examples of similar attitudes and behaviour, and goes on to claim that God acts justly and justifies his acts to men. They refer briefly to the folly of atheists, and the perplexity of doubters of God's justice, who become ever more muddled in difficulties they themselves create, trying to bind God to laws he made for men, not for himself. But God is infinite and may operate his laws as he wishes; if he wishes, he may grant Jews dispensation from the law which forbids them to marry non-Jews – as clearly he did for Samson

NOTES AND GLOSSARY:

never was there School: there never was any organised group (of atheists)

national obstriction: a general rule applying to a whole nation

Nazarite: Samson was a member of this very strict Jewish sect thought of as sacred and especially dear to God

purity: Samson was 'impure' in wanting to marry an 'unclean' and non-Jewish foreigner. This seems to be not Dalila but the woman of Timnath who married another after being married to him

---

Lines 326–651 The second Episode: Samson and Manoa

At this point Manoa, Samson's old father, appears. He also laments the suffering and degradation of his son, and sadly recalls how he had

prayed for a son, and been overjoyed when Samson was born and
proved so splendid. He chides God, saying that God should not so
punish for mistakes of ordinary human weakness a man whom he has
chosen for special great purposes.

Lines 373–419
Samson, however, tells his father not to blame God, and takes full
responsibility for his present state, again rebuking himself for betraying
God's secret (of the source of his strength) to an enemy woman. Again
he tells of the two women who betrayed him, this time recounting in
greater detail the story of Dalila's treachery. He concludes by asserting
that his present servitude is less base than his former servitude to the
women, his past blindness worse than his present.

Lines 420–71
Manoa does not minimise Samson's past error and stresses how bitterly
he is paying for it. But, he says, worse is to come, for the Philistines are
today celebrating their god Dagon, as responsible for getting Samson
into their power, and will be scorning and demeaning God, which must
cause Samson the heaviest suffering and shame he could feel. Samson
readily acknowledges this responsibility, and this anguish. The only
consolation he can find is that he is finished with; there will now be direct
confrontation of God by Dagon, and Dagon must and will be overcome.

Lines 472–520
Manoa is equally confident about this. He goes on to tell his son that he
has approached some Philistine lords about the possibility of a ransom
for Samson. But Samson rejects this possibility; he wants to pay in full
by suffering for his crime – of shameful talkativeness, revealing God's
holy secret. However, Manoa persists, telling him to repent the sin but to
accept being let off the penalty if this is offered. Perhaps God will relent;
he is always pleased if men are humble and penitent. He should leave it
to God to decide, not try to decide it himself, which would be a kind of
self-indulgence, and would suggest that Samson is more displeased with
his offence against himself than with his sin against God. Who knows
what God has decided; perhaps it is that you shall return home, he says.

Lines 521–76
Samson replies that he implores God's pardon, but he is not sure that he
wants to prolong his own life. Again he harps on the great exploits for
which he had been intended and the present miserable reality brought
about by his pride and sensuality which put him in the power of Dalila.
    The Chorus tries to soften his self-reproach, declaring that he had
been temperate in the matter of drink. But Samson does not see much
virtue in that since he had been weak in other ways and he again reviles
himself and draws a picture of his humiliated self and hopeless future.

Lines 577–605

Manoa asks him if then he will continue to help the Philistines whom he was intended to harm. It would be better for him to lie idle at home. He goes on to wonder if God may not still have a purpose in mind for Samson, might not even restore his sight; pointing out that Samson has regained his miraculous strength. But the latter has no hope left at all, and Manoa, urging him not to listen to his own black despair, goes off to do more to secure his son's liberation if he can.

Lines 606–51

Samson bemoans the fact that his torment is not only bodily; his mental torment is even more grievous. Yet again he dwells on the past hopes for him and his present plight.

NOTES AND GLOSSARY:

Canaanite:	the Philistines were immigrants settled in the land of Canaan, that is, Palestine west of the River Jordan; the term Canaanite was used generally for the enemies of Israel
capital:	a three-way pun: to do with the head (Latin, *caput*); principal; fatal
a sin . . . condemn:	Samson refers to the classical story of Tantalus, condemned to everlasting punishment in Hell for revealing to men the secrets of the gods. Pride lay at the bottom of his crime: he wished to be known to men as one familiar with the gods
swollen with pride:	Samson acknowledges his sin of pride
wether:	a castrated ram

Lines 652–709 The second Stasimon

The Chorus concludes this section with a long meditation on patience and fortitude, on how difficult it is for a man to accept suffering if he lacks the consolation of faith, and on the strange workings of God's will. Sometimes he casts down even his most chosen, and his actions seem inconsistent. They call on God to continue so to treat his once glorious champion.

Lines 710–1009 The third Episode: Samson and Dalila

At this point, Samson's treacherous wife Dalila arrives in glorious finery and heavily scented but with a show of sorrow. She says she has come hesitantly and penitently, wondering if she can make any amends. Samson rebuffs her angrily, not believing in her sincerity. She persists in trying to excuse her past actions, saying that it was feminine curiosity that led her. She goes on to say that he should not have given way. There was human weakness on both sides, and she asks him to forgive hers. For, she continues, her motive was fear of losing him, and she had told the secret of the source of his strength to the Philistine leaders so that he would no longer be called out on dangerous exploits but, enfeebled, be able to stay at home with her. Samson rebuts this cunning argument. He acknowledges his own weakness and says he pardons her weakness as far as he pardons his own, but calls on her to look at herself truthfully and she will then see the falseness of her present quest. He disposes, too, of her argument about being motivated by love: if it was anything it was lust. And how could she have hoped for love from someone she had betrayed and in whom she was bound to have provoked eternal hatred?

Dalila now adopts a different defence, telling of the pressure put upon her by the Philistine leaders to help to trap an enemy as a public and religious duty, and of how in the end she put public good before private. Samson angrily mocks this hypocritical claim. He had genuinely loved her, he says, and had been accepted; he was not an enemy then. And how can she call it religious duty, as she had? What gods they are, the gods of the Philistines, if they can only work in such ungodly ways.

Dalila makes a last attempt to win Samson back, saying she will plead with the Philistine lords for him to be allowed to be freed to go back home where she will lovingly tend him. But Samson is not to be deceived by her any more and angrily dismisses her. She leaves after defiantly declaring that her name will ever be the most famous among her people for her loyal service, and she will be publicly honoured and rewarded.

NOTES AND GLOSSARY:

Female ... play: in Giles Fletcher's *Christ's Victory on Earth* (1610) the personification Presumption comes to tempt Christ; she is presented as vain and painted, moving like a fine sailing-ship

Javan ... Gadire: Greece and Cadiz

With doubtful ... misdeed: in Euripides's *The Trojan Women*, Helen of Troy, fearful but having adorned herself, attempts to excuse her unfaithfulness to her angry husband Menelaus with lies and sentimental pleas

Hyaena: known for cowardly guile, and believed to be able to lure men by imitating the human voice

enchanted cup and warbling charms: he sees Dalila now as an enchantress like Circe

Ecron ... Gath: with Askelon, the chief cities of the Philistines

Not less renowned ... nailed: in the Bible, Judges 4, Jael, wife of Heber, offered the Canaanite leader, Sisera, hospitality and killed him in his sleep, in the Mount Ephraim region of Canaan

piety:	sense of duty and devotion (to family or country) (Latin, *pietas*)

Lines 1010–60 The third Stasimon

There follows a brief discussion about the power of love and then the Chorus talks about love-betrayal, female weakness, male disillusionment with women and the rarity of happy marriage, concluding with the statement that this is why God gave men despotic power over women. (There is clearly much of Milton's personal feeling expressed.)

NOTES AND GLOSSARY:
paranymph: 'best man', or groomsman at a wedding
Is it for that . . . nor dismayed: this discussion of woman's frailty and unhappiness in marriage and God's decreeing of despotic power accordingly to man owes much to Milton's own unhappy marital experience. His *Divorce Tractates* of 1643–5 expound on the subject, and there are many references and comments in *Paradise Lost*, especially in relation to Eve's behaviour

---
Lines 1061–267 The fourth Episode: Samson and Harapha

Now comes the giant Harapha, to see, as he says, the great fighter Samson of whom he has heard. He regrets that he has never had the chance of fighting him and never will, now that Samson is blind. Samson rejoins that Harapha's masters had not dared to contend with him openly, but only by trickery through his treacherous wife. He challenges him now, as heavily armed and armoured as he wishes, to single combat. Harapha suspects Samson still has secret powers, but Samson denies this, saying he trusts only in the living God. Let them fight, Harapha as the champion of the Philistine god Dagon, and then see which God is stronger. Harapha contemptuously taunts Samson saying that the latter's God has already given him up, and would not accept Samson, a murderer, revolter and thief, as his champion. In reply, Samson tells yet again of his having chosen a Philistine wife and of her betrayal of him, and justifies his past actions against the Philistine enemy. He again challenges Harapha, who again contemptuously refuses and the scene ends with insulting speeches from both.

The Chorus fears that Harapha will stir up the leaders to bring further affliction to Samson, but the latter does not fear this, thinking there is nothing worse they can do except something which would make him incapable of working for them. He says that his deadliest enemy would prove his best friend by doing him to death.

NOTES AND GLOSSARY:

Harapha:	the name means 'the Giant'. The incident is not in Judges, although elsewhere (2 Samuel 21) Philistine champions are called 'the sons of Rapha'
Og... Anak:	giants in the Old Testament
Tongue-doughty:	brave in words
Baal-zebub:	god of flies, worshipped by the Philistines
Astaroth:	the moon-goddess of the Canaanites
five sons:	in 2 Samuel 21 'the giant in Gath' has four sons. Milton adds Goliath, the most famous biblical giant, who was overthrown by David

Lines 1268–96 The fourth Stasimon

The Chorus recognises and praises the return of some strength and heroic certainty to Samson. They speak of two kinds of moral strength: that of heroes who can deliver their people from oppression, and that of saints who suffer and endure. Samson may be either of these. He has heroic 'magnitude', but, now blinded, it may be that heroic patience and fortitude are to be his destiny.

Lines 1297–426 The fifth Episode: Samson and the officer

An officer now comes with an order for Samson to appear at Dagon's feast to demonstrate his great strength, but the hero replies that as a Hebrew he is forbidden to attend other religious rites, and refuses. The officer warns him of the offence his refusal will give, but Samson is firm and when the officer has gone, and the Chorus has expressed anxiety at the outcome, he stoutly declares that he will not use his now returning God-given strength in this contemptible and profane way. He then says he feels a mounting excitement within him, and a feeling that this day will see something remarkable; and he resolves to go.

At this moment the officer returns, threateningly demanding his appearance at the festival, and Samson agrees, pretending that he complies because he has no alternative. He takes leave of the Chorus, not wishing them to accompany him because he thinks the crowd on this their holy day will be in violent mood. He departs, saying that whatever is going to happen, they will not hear of any dishonourable action discreditable to God, the Hebrew law and nation or himself.

Lines 1427–40 The fifth Stasimon

They wish him well, invoking both God and the angel who had come down to foretell his birth and great deeds.

Lines 1441–end The Exode (catastrophe or conclusion), which includes the Kommos

Manoa suddenly appears; he has come to tell them how he has been getting on in his attempt to secure the ransom of his son. He is interrupted by a great noise, but goes on again, imagining how he will pay the ransom and look after his son. He feels, as Samson's strength has returned with the growing of his hair, that God still has some great purpose for Samson, and may even restore his sight as well. There comes another greater noise, which Manoa calls 'hideous', and the Chorus a 'universal groan' betokening ruin and destruction. Manoa fears they have slain his son; the Chorus thinks that it is Samson who is slaughtering Philistines, and wonders whether perhaps his sight has been restored and this is helping him in his death-dealing.

Lines 1541–95
A messenger comes, in fearful flight. It is some little time – thirty lines of exchanges between him and Manoa – before he can manage to say that Samson is dead. It takes nearly thirty more anguished lines before the messenger can begin his account of what happened.

Lines 1596–659
The messenger describes the scene, and the arrival of Samson in a procession, wearing the uniform of a public servant. He was brought to a place to perform stupendous tasks, all of which he patiently did. Then, to give him a rest, he was led to a point between the two great pillars which held up the vault. He was given permission to lean on the pillars with both arms outstretched and he seemed to pray, or to be thinking deeply. At last he held up his head and spoke, saying to the Philistine lords that he had done what they had asked of him, and was now going to show even greater and more amazing strength. At that, gathering all his great power, he bent over, tugging the two pillars till they fell, and the roof with them, all the lords and he himself dying in the collapsing building.

Lines 1660–707 The Kommos: threnody or lament in which the Chorus and one actor – or more – unite
The Chorus glories in this fulfilment of the prophecies. Then one half, a Semichorus, interprets the event as one in which God had made a spirit of frenzy in the feasting Philistines, drunk with idolatry, wine and sacrificial meat, worshipping their idol. In that frenzy, they had called, unwittingly, for their destined destroyer. The other Semichorus thinks and speaks of the glorious revival of Samson:

> His fiery virtue rous'd
> From under ashes into sudden flame

Lines 1708–end
Manoa is reconciled to the event and proud of the heroic revenge
enacted by his son and of his noble death. There is nothing to mourn for,
he says. It is clear that God had not, after all, abandoned Samson. He
proposes that they should go to find and cleanse his body and prepare
for the funeral; he will build him a noble monument, on which his great
deeds will be recorded. And the Chorus ends with a short speech
declaring that all is ordained by God for the best, even if it seems that
sometimes he hides his face. His faithful followers have been given new
knowledge by this happening and are discharged by him in peace and
calm and consolation.

NOTES AND GLOSSARY:

cataphracts:	men and their horses both fully armoured
Silo:	Shiloh, sixty-five miles north-east of Gaza, where the Ark of the Covenant was kept and where at times 'the glory of the Lord filled the Tabernacle' (Exodus 40)
Dragon:	serpent
villatic:	farmyard (Latin, *villa*, a farm)
self-begotten bird:	the phoenix, a unique legendary Arabian bird which, after living for five hundred years, is burned in its nest by the sun's heat, a new bird immediately arising from the ashes

Part 3

Commentary

'On the Morning of Christ's Nativity'

Written when Milton was just twenty-one, and begun at dawn on Christmas Day 1629, as he wrote to his friend Diodati, the so-called 'Hymn', more commonly called the 'Nativity Ode', was his first great English poem. He had written more in Latin than in English up to this time. In his 6th Elegy, written in Latin at the same time, to Charles Diodati, he ended:

> I am writing a poem about the king who was born of heavenly seed, and who brought peace to men. I am writing about the blessed ages promised in Holy Scripture, about the infant cries of God, about the stabling under a poor roof of Him who dwells with his Father in the highest heavens, about the sky's giving birth to a new star, about the hosts who sang in the air, and about the pagan gods suddenly shattered in their own shrines. These are the gifts I have given for Christ's birthday: the first light of the dawn brought them to me.*

This account economically sketches the content of the poem and incidentally points to the contrasts and paradoxes in it. The paradoxes of course exist in the Scripture story: God become man, Father become child, King of Heaven born in a poor stable on earth, angels coming to celebrate and pagan gods vanishing in disarray; Milton's emphasis on them in the poem accounts for one of its remarkable qualities – a breathtaking sense of surprise.

Of course it was not an entirely original poem, fresh though it is. There had been numerous nativity poems, in Latin and in Italian and French as well as in English. Very few had combined the elements – the child born in a stable in poverty, the angels attending and singing the Christ child's praises, the ending of the power of classical oracles, the contrast between the innocent babe and Christ the future Saviour and Judge – as Milton did. John Carey in his notes to the poem defines a big debt to the Italian poem 'On the Day of the Nativity' by Torquato Tasso (published in his *Rime* in 1621), and close similarity to some passages in the early Christian Latin poet Prudentius (born AD348). But Milton was still a young poet, and it was, and is, natural for a young poet to turn to and imitate his predecessors. That is the obvious way to learn how to be

*Translation from John Carey in *Milton*, Longmans Annotated English Poets, 1968.

a poet. Although the poem is close to Tasso's in many details including the emphasis on the humbleness of the birth-place, the universal peace at the time of the nativity, and the flight of Apollo, the Egyptian animal gods and the false gods of the pagans, most of these were common elements in the nativity story, but Milton almost certainly remembered Tasso's poem as he wrote. Many details, too, might have been familiar because they are shown so often in late medieval and Renaissance painting. Anyone who has received a Christmas card reproducing a nativity scene from an illuminated manuscript or a painting from this time will know how common were many of the ingredients of the story. And of course the actual events of the nativity – the star, the stable, the manger, the Magi with presents, the shepherds – were universally known from the Scriptures to a church-going population, used to celebrating Christmas Day.

What is uncommon is the tone of the poem, its elegant, light, almost jaunty view of the stupendous event it celebrates, and its freshness and variety. Although Milton writes grandly of Nature being in awe, of the silence and peace into which the whole world fell at the moment of the birth of Jesus Christ, he also writes of meek-eyed Peace sliding down to earth like a classical goddess – or a figure in a Jacobean masque – and of the Sun slowing down his progress and hiding his head for shame because his light was now to be far outshone by Christ, the Light of the World. This fanciful exaggeration comes again later in the poem when he writes of the flight of all the pagan gods at the birth of Christ.

Clearly it is a Christian poem, but it is written in the imaginative terms of classical epic and mythology. The combination – of classical and Christian – will be found in Milton's work throughout his career, and the poems dealt with in these notes well illustrate it. Furthermore, while always conscious of the divinely ordained event – the birth of Jesus Christ; God coming to earth to be born as a human child – and of the greatness of its effect on human history, the young poet cannot but respond to the simplicity of it as well as to the wonder and glory. It is this remarkable combination especially which gives greatness to the poem.

Milton probably learned something of it from Edmund Spenser, the English poet he most admired. In a very few lines of 'An Hymne to Heavenlie Love' the Elizabethan poet captures a tone of simplicity and innocence as he describes the saviour of the world 'encradled' in 'simple cratch, wrapt in a wad of hay', as elsewhere in the poem he finely suggests the sublimity of God's love and Christ's sacrifice. There is a stylistic debt too. Milton's stanzas both in the introduction and in the 'Hymn' each conclude with an alexandrine (the twelve-syllabled, six-stress line with which the so-called Spenserian stanza, in which Spenser's great poem *The Faerie Queene* was written, ends). Here and there they are reminiscent of Spenser in their phrasing – 'a darksome house of mortal clay'; 'All the spangled host keep watch in squadrons bright'; 'secret altar touch'd with hallow'd fire'. The form of the poem is also in debt to Spenser. It was he who first wrote in English celebratory poems in a free form of rhymed verse using long and shorter lines reminiscent of classical odes – celebratory songs. Milton's stanzas here are firmer and more regular than Spenser's: each stanza of the 'Hymn' rhymes *aab ccb dd*, and is lightly divided, therefore, into three units, two triplets and a couplet. It is also reminiscent of the Italian *canzone* tradition with its pattern of long and short lines. The English stanza of Spenser and Milton is always shorter than the Italian one, and its syllables are ten and six, rather than eleven and seven, giving five and three stresses respectively. The direct influence of Tasso, too, in this respect, and in the tone of voice, is apparent, though Milton's tone is lighter.

When you first read this poem on such a holy subject you will probably be surprised at this. You may feel it is inappropriate for the subject matter. Great natural phenomena like light, night and the sun are presented as classical gods, sometimes with all too human touches (such as the sun behind the red curtains of a four-poster bed pillowing his chin). The pagan gods with their dreadful rites and powers at times seem rather like demons in a children's story, especially the followers of Moloch 'in dismal dance' to the clanging of cymbals 'about the furnace blue', or as they 'shriek' and 'moan' and 'sigh'. The radiance and heavenly music of the angelic host are matters for rapture and wonder. Indeed, the whole poem seems almost magical, almost breathtaking, indeed almost breathless with wonder. Can you imagine a child gasping with excitement, amazement and awe at some great spectacle, or at something unbelievably beautiful? That is the impression of Milton's reaction to the nativity which can be got from this poem. Elation and happiness are also there, appropriately, for he is singing of the certainty of future ages of happiness because of the birth of Jesus.

Yet if you look again, you see that although it is cast in this imaginative way, and the verse-form creates a light, singing, dancing movement throughout, Milton has not failed to suggest the grand cosmic significance of the event. Nor has he failed to make clear the vileness of the superstitious pagan religions. They are shown as both horrible and contemptible, frightening and in the last resort trivial.

In the four-stanza introduction (the stanza of Chaucer's *Troilus and Criseyde* and some of the *Canterbury Tales* and of Spenser's *Four Hymnes*, though Milton makes the seventh and last line the longer alexandrine), the poet had written of the 'happy morn' of the birth of Jesus and had called on the Heavenly Muse to welcome him with some 'verse . . . hymn or solemn strain'. The 'Hymn' that follows is far from solemn. Serious it may be, but it is also fanciful and jubilant, a truly celebratory ode.

'L'Allegro' and 'Il Penseroso'

These are obviously companion-pieces. They present two ways of looking at and enjoying life – cheerful or thoughtful and serious, which is roughly what the two Italian words mean. Although they are presented in contrast, there is no deliberate conflict between them. They are 'tone-poems', as it were, not merely opposing arguments in a debate. Both discuss virtuous pleasures in life, both are relaxed and light-hearted, although of course the pensive man's pleasures are more studious. There is a lot of contrasting: day and night; social and solitary; comedy and tragedy; court and cloister; song and hymn or secular and sacred music. A modern addition, not without justice, might be extrovert and introvert.

'L'Allegro' and 'Il Penseroso' are delicate, fanciful poems, which deliberately emulate in various ways and often echo the poetry of Shakespeare and of Ben Jonson, and share something of Spenser's sensuous use of language (for example, 'Il Penseroso' lines 126–54) and his onomatopoeia (using words which suggest in their sound the things they are describing). Yet although they are poetical exercises and do not touch deep thought or emotion, they discuss and incidentally reveal two strains in Milton's nature and suggest in brief a contention in his mind which many critics find. The sensuous and pleasure-loving contends with the serious and Puritan; the fanciful Elizabethan poet in him with the poet dedicated to an epic and almost prophetic role. The debate in *Comus* is an exaggerated example of it; the passage in 'Lycidas' in which the poet questions his own decision to live a life dedicated to learning and serious writing touches upon it (lines 64–84); even in *Paradise Lost* and *Samson Agonistes* there is still something of the tension remaining, in the temptations to Eve and then by Eve to Adam, and by Manoa and Dalila to Samson. The two ways of living and of looking at life are also memorably discussed in two of Milton's Latin poems to his old school friend Charles Diodati.

The poems do not exactly correspond, as 'Il Penseroso' is twenty-four lines longer. But the movement of the arguments corresponds, and metrically they are identical. Both begin with a ten-line introduction (in each case the subject of which is the sending away of the 'rival' goddess) of alternating six-syllabled and ten-syllabled lines rhyming *abba cdde ec*. This derives no doubt from the Italian *canzone* alternation of seven and eleven. Both then move into light, free, eight-syllabled lines, varied irregularly with seven-syllabled lines, of which there are twice as many (thirty-two per cent) in 'L'Allegro' as in 'Il Penseroso': fittingly, since the subject matter is of lighter pleasures. These dancing octosyllabics ensure that the reader receives and enjoys these delightful poems in the playful, relaxed spirit in which they were written.

Comus

Milton and his friend the musician Henry Lawes (an official of the Chapel Royal and one of the King's Musicians) collaborated in the creating of *A Masque Presented at Ludlow Castle* in honour of the installation of the Earl of Bridgewater as President of the Council of Wales and Lord Lieutenant of Wales and the Border counties in September 1634. (It was not named *Comus* until it was adapted for the eighteenth-century stage in 1738.) Although called *A Masque*, and more like a masque than anything else, it is not a typical masque, chiefly because of its length and scale and because of the seriousness of its argument. The *Masque* had been for a century a popular entertainment at court and in great houses. Originally, as its name suggests, it had consisted chiefly of 'masquing', in which some guests entered wearing masks, acting in dumbshow and dancing. (This had itself grown from an Italian custom – see Shakespeare's *Romeo and Juliet*, in which Juliet first meets Romeo when he comes to her father's feast masked, with a group of masked friends.) Before long, shape was given to the combination of music, dance and song by making a small dramatic action or argument, and from this the Elizabethan court masque developed, being used especially to pay elaborate compliments to the queen and to show the triumphs of virtue. Once plot and argument had come, the masque could and did become more elaborate and serious in subject matter; Ben Jonson especially, in the reign of James I, included more learning, more moral discussion, and also allegory – in which ideas, feelings, emotions, teaching are presented not directly but in a disguised but recognisable form – as well as more elaborate settings and stage-machinery.

In *Comus* the chief element is neither of these, nor is it music or dance, but a dramatic plot. A young girl is separated from her brothers and lost in a wood. She is captured and unsuccessfully tempted by a wicked enchanter, Comus, is rescued by her brothers and released from the enchanted seat by the goddess of the nearby River Severn. All then proceed to the castle of the girl's and her brothers' parents, where they are reunited. This plot, of some dramatic tension, seems itself to matter less to Milton than the argument which he develops at the centre of the action in the temptation scene: between temperance and intemperance, chastity and sensuality, morality and immorality.

But *Comus* is a masque in a number of senses:

(1) It is a colourful stage spectacle with fine costumes, changes of costume and some fairly elaborate stage effects: the rising of Sabrina, attended by water-nymphs, for example, and the changes of scene by changing painted back-drops.

(2) It includes a number of songs and some dances, and in performance there was other music as well.

(3) It contains characteristic opposition of virtue and vice.

(4) It makes use of mythological figures and much mythological reference.

(5) It pays compliments to an honoured person or family: indeed, in this case, the whole piece is an extended compliment to the Earl and his family.

(6) It contains a sort of 'Antimasque', which, in masques at least since Ben Jonson established a common masque form in the early seventeenth century, came first. It provided a contrast between the courtly characters and characters of rural or low life, or grotesque creatures of the imagination (satyrs and witches, for example): here, Comus's rout of strange dancing followers with animal heads. *Comus* has a strong pastoral element. The Attendant Spirit disguises himself as a shepherd, and so does Comus himself; there are many references to country life – sheep, shepherds, grazing – and there is a contrast implicit between the simple virtues of pastoral life and Comus's corrupt 'court' and followers. And the 'court' at Ludlow Castle to which the three young people are eventually brought is a place of virtue, and the dance of shepherds in this scene emphasises simplicity and innocence. Some have found this to suggest that *Comus* is really not so much a masque as a pastoral drama (like Tasso's *Aminta* and Guarini's *Pastor Fido* – both Italian of the sixteenth century).

Another source or influence is in fact indicated, in the work of one of Milton's favourite poets, Edmund Spenser. In his poetry, especially in his great epic and romantic narrative *The Faerie Queene* (1590 and 1596), may be found:

(1) Pastoral used and by implication praised as a 'type' of virtue often in contrast with its opposite at courts.

(2) Varied woodland and country settings.

(3) A combination of rural and courtly, real and fanciful, mythological and allegorical characters – gods and nymphs, witches and enchanters, deceivers and deceived.

(4) The whole imaginative narrative creation serving a clear moral purpose, one basically Christian but also of course indebted to classical moral philosophy.

Much of this is a common literary heritage, but the direct influence of Spenser was great.

In addition, much of the actual material in *Comus* derives closely from *The Faerie Queene* (but Spenser himself drew much from Italian romantic epic, especially from Ariosto and Tasso, whose work Milton also knew).

(1)   Comus appears as a humble servant and offers the Lady hospitality in a cottage. (The enchanter Archimago in *The Faerie Queene* Book I, deceives the Lady Una and her knight.)
(2)   Comus has the power, derived from his mother Circe, to turn men into lustful beasts. (Acrasia the enchantress in her Bower of Bliss in Book II is a Circe-figure with this power.)
(3)   The virtuous Lady is seized by the enchanter Comus. (Amoret is so seized by Busirane in Book III, although the circumstances are quite different.)
(4)   Comus attempts to make the Lady, held by magic in a chair, submit to his will. (Amoret in the House of Busirane in Book III.)
(5)   She is freed from the enchantment by the superior power of a virtuous lady. (Britomart's freeing of Amoret in Book III.)
(6)   The Lady is an example, almost a symbol, of virtue and chastity. (The twin sisters Amoret and Belphoebe and the lady-knight Britomart represent different aspects of love, virginity, and unmarried and married chastity in Books III and IV, and there are a number of others elsewhere in the poem.)

Milton cannot have been more than twenty-five when *Comus* was written, and it is only natural that it should have been influenced by other writers. It is a compilation, not a genuinely original creation, but then the form of masque is an artificial one anyway. Milton like Spenser shows the dual nature of much Renaissance culture, combining classical and mythological with Christian elements. This is most prominent in the central argument of *Comus*, which is both a Christian – almost a Puritan – and a Platonic upholding of the virtues of moderation and self-discipline. Milton wrote in one of his prose pamphlets on Church matters (*An Apology for Smectymnuus*) of his debt 'to the divine volumes of *Plato* . . .' where he learned:

> of chastity and love . . . whose charming cup is only vertue which she bears in her hand to those who are worthy. The rest are cheated with a thick intoxicating potion which a certaine Sorceresse the abuser of loves name carries about . . . The first and chiefest office of love, begins and ends in the soule, producing those happy twins of her divine generation knowledge and vertue.

The Platonic view that the soul is immortal, and can attain happiness only in the ascent from earthly things towards the knowledge and love of God, is several times expressed in *Comus*, chiefly by the Elder Brother (lines 359–475, especially lines 373–85, and in lines 453–75) but also by the Lady (lines 210–20).

Milton has sometimes been criticised for giving the Lady a comparatively weak defence (lines 756–99) in response to Comus's powerful argument in urging her not to 'hoard' her virginity but to make full and joyful use of her bodily beauty (lines 706–55). However, it can be argued that it was wise not to concentrate the whole counter-argument in one speech by one person, and not to give too much intellectual weight to the character of the heroine at this point in the drama. 'Tough' heroines can lose sympathy, and we must not lose sympathy with this beautiful, threatened young girl. Milton has entrusted to other characters, especially the Elder Brother, the chief burden of argument, and indeed had made the audience (or reader) aware from the very beginning, in the Attendant Spirit's opening speech, of what the virtuous argument was, and of its attractiveness. If this were primarily a drama, it might well be criticised for the weakness of its climax – the confrontation and conflict of Comus and the Lady, tempter and resister, excess and moderation, evil and good. However it is not primarily a drama, but an imaginative entertainment elegantly presenting an interesting argument.

This is not to say that it is without dramatic effect and could not be successfully staged. There are quite dramatic scenes and scenes of quite thrilling contrast. Almost every time the character or characters on stage hear or sense the approach of someone else there is drama. The sudden irruption on to the stage of Comus and his beast-headed followers is a good dramatic surprise. In a quite opposite way, the stage quietness into which the Lady sings her song, and the immediately subsequent appearance on stage of Comus himself, hushed by the beauty of the song, are dramatically effective. Do not forget, either, the theatrical effect of darkness and people moving in dim light, or the moving effect of music in the theatre.

But at its original performance in September 1634 high drama would not have been expected of it. It was a festive occasion. The Lady and her two brothers were played by the young daughter and the two young sons (they were aged fifteen, eleven and nine at the time) of the Earl in whose honour it was staged at his Castle. The composer himself, Henry Lawes, played the part of the Attendant Spirit. The message, the sentiments, the reciting, the costumes and the music were more important than the drama of the piece.

A criticism is that there seems to be some confusion in *Comus* between chastity and virginity. The Lady first mentions chastity (line 215). It is an unexpected use. Lost in the wood, in fear and danger, she had cried a welcome, as it were, to Faith and Hope:

O, welcome, pure ey'd Faith, white-handed Hope.

She then interrupts herself with a parenthesis about Hope:

(thou hovering Angel girt with golden wings);

and then, when we are expecting mention of the third of the biblical trio, Charity, she instead adds

And thou unblemish'd form of Chastity!

It is a clever device of Milton's, for it invests 'chastity' in our imaginations with some of the wider range of association and greater virtue of 'charity'. In the next scene (line 420), the Elder Brother refers to his sister's chastity, her 'hidden strength', and makes three other references to chastity. But he also, in the same speech, mentions 'virgin purity' and 'true virginity'.

When we get to the actual temptation scene (for that is what it is, although the Lady is not in fact in any danger of being tempted), there is no doubt that what Comus wants is the surrender of her virginity. He wants her to drink the magic potion which will give her animal lusts and lack of restraint. The argument covers larger ground than this, and becomes a general debate on discipline versus indulgence, the spiritual versus the bodily, but towards the end of her defence, the Lady again speaks of both 'the sun-clad power of Chastity' and 'the sage and serious doctrine of Virginity'.

Sometimes it looks as if virginity and chastity are being used interchangeably. If so, that would be a surprising weakness. We have also to take into account the last speech of the masque, by the Attendant Spirit, which celebrates not virginity nor even chastity, but the well-being of Adonis, god of love, and the marriage of Cupid and Psyche, and their future children. Because the plot is about an attempt upon the virtue of a young virgin, the greater emphasis seems to be on virginity. In fact that is only because the idea of chastity can be given greater dramatic force in the situation of a virgin threatened by a sensualist than in any other way in a drama. Milton is not commending virginity simply for its own sake, but because it is a kind of chastity and therefore a kind of virtue. It is virtue because in it the spiritual and aspiring part of human nature is shown to be stronger than the physical. But it is not negative, as Comus claims, because it is part of a whole virtuous way of living, and this is perhaps why Milton has earlier played his word-trick (Faith, Hope and *Chastity* – to emphasise the positive and loving aspect of the virtue) and why he ends with a sort of vision of happy, fruitful marriage far above even 'the happy climes' to which the Attendant Spirit returns.

In short, the particular instance Milton chose was the predicament of a virgin in danger, but his general concern was with what makes for virtuous behaviour. And that is self-control; reason and knowledge controlling passion and instinct. We find this theme in many places in Milton's work, especially in *Paradise Lost* and *Samson Agonistes*.

The Masque also presents a journey – a little journey, it is true – of young, virtuous souls through the dark wood of life (the darkness represents danger and temptation). The Lady wins through; and her victory, the victory of virtue and purity, marks a vital stage in a human's development. The noble parents to whom she and her brothers are safely restored – real parents of real children at that first performance on Michaelmas Night (29 September 1634) at Ludlow Castle – must have been pleased with the lesson and its imaginative presentation by Milton and Lawes.

Style

Comus is written chiefly but not exclusively in five-stressed blank (that is, unrhymed ten-syllabled) verse. There are some passages in heroic couplets (the dialogue between the Attendant Spirit and the Elder Brother – lines 495–512); some *stichomythia* (the line-for-line interchange between the Lady and Comus disguised as a shepherd – lines 277–90); and some use of the four-stressed rhyming couplet common to most masques in Comus's first speech, in the Attendant Spirit's exchanges with Sabrina and in his final speech (lines 867–1023). Of the songs, some are in couplets, some in irregular unrhymed verse.

It is a successful and varied piece of writing; it is only the *stichomythia* which perhaps does not really succeed. The blank verse, used for all the serious exposition and discussion of the piece, is on the whole free and flexible, and Milton already shows considerable mastery of the verse-paragraph which was so important for successful handling of lofty narrative and speech. He achieves flexibility in a number of ways:

(1) By varying the placing of the stress or emphasis, and of the *caesura* or pause in lines.

(2) By much use of lines which run on without pause from the line or lines before, making for good pace and flow – *enjambement*.

(3) By much use of feminine endings (an extra unstressed syllable – lines 8 and 10 are examples).

In the writing of blank verse, Milton was naturally much influenced by Marlowe, Shakespeare and other Elizabethan dramatists, and there are echoes, perhaps unconscious, of Shakespearean and other phrases, images and metaphors. But again, probably the greatest debt was to Spenser, with whom he felt not only a moral but a literary affinity. (Dryden reported Milton as having said that Spenser was his 'original' – which in the seventeenth century meant 'ancestor' or 'father' as well as 'source' or 'model'.) Spenser did not write in blank verse, so there is no formal debt, but the influence is undeniable and strong. As F. T. Prince* has pointed out, Milton would have studied his poetry at St

The Italian Element in Milton's Verse, Oxford, 1954.

Paul's School, London, for the headmaster made much use of quotations from Spenser in his teaching of English grammar and rhetoric. Milton would have had to analyse Spenser's poetic diction as a school exercise, and there is no doubt that he learned in detail from the older poet how to write poetry in English that corresponded to Virgil's style, how to make the sound of the poetry express and suggest the sense, how to use words, sounds and images to convey vividly the appropriate feeling and emotional value so that the reader is moved – to joy, fear, revulsion, sorrow and so on.

Finally it may be said that the verse is successful in suggesting speech, although it is usually formal rather than intensely dramatic speech, and so appropriate to the formality of a masque entertainment.

Comus contains some of the most beautiful of all Milton's writing: in Comus's first speech, a delicate, sensuous, imaginative vision of fairyland, like Spenser's or like Shakespeare's in *A Midsummer Night's Dream*; sweet passages of description of nature (lines 311–18), or evocation of it (lines 494–507); descriptions of romantic landscapes (lines 421–46, 520–50); the ardently powerful and imaginative speech of Comus, evoking a grand sense of the richness of the created world, in lines 710–36. There is lightness and variety and simplicity, for Milton also profited from the example of Ben Jonson, in his masques and in his other verse. The young Milton wrote some of the most imaginative, fanciful and harmonious of all English poetry, and *Comus* is his major achievement of this kind.

'Lycidas'

A fellow-student of Milton at Christ's College, Cambridge, who had become a Fellow (full teaching member) of the college, Edward King, was drowned off the coast of North Wales on 10 August 1637. The ship he was travelling in hit a rock. While others tried to save themselves, King knelt in prayer and went down when the ship sank. In the following year, 1638, a volume of memorial verses in Latin, Greek and English was published by King's friends and acquaintances, of whom Milton was one. His poem, the last in the volume, was 'Lycidas'.

To anyone who knew the literature of the time well, the name itself would show the sort of poem it was. A shepherd named Lycidas was 'best at playing the pipes' in *Idylls* 7 by Theocritus. (An idyll – the Greek word means 'little picture' – was a small idealised story, usually in verse and pastoral in setting.) Theocritus was a writer of Greek descent living in Sicily in the third century BC. The beginning and growth of this form of poetic writing generally known as 'pastoral' (from the Latin *pastor* meaning a shepherd), but sometimes known as 'bucolic' (from the Greek word for a herdsman), is due to Theocritus. One of those who followed him, Bion (c. 100BC), also uses the name Lycidas, as does the later Roman poet Virgil (70–19BC) in his *Eclogues* (7 and 9). ('Eclogue', literally meaning 'selection', is the name commonly given to a pastoral poem.)

The subject matter of pastoral poetry is the days and ways of idealised shepherds, an ideal world of innocence and, generally, of happiness in the simple life and simple activities. The shepherds represent good, virtuous men, almost without exception. They also represent, or are, virtuous lovers. In addition, they almost always represent poets. They 'sing' or write happy songs about the good life, they have singing competitions, they discuss the flocks and the seasons, they talk about love; sometimes they lament unhappiness in love. Sometimes they 'sing' an 'elegy' (the Greek word for a mourning-song) for a dead shepherd. The first idyll of Theocritus contains the 'Lament for Daphnis' a shepherd who died for love. It starts: 'Begin, ye Muses dear, begin the pastoral song! Thyrsis of Etna am I . . . where ah! where were ye when Daphnis was languishing; ye Nymphs, where were ye?' It inspired and became the model for most of the great pastoral elegies from Bion's 'Lament for Adonis' and the 'Lament for Bion' (probably by one Moschus) to Spenser's 'November Eclogue' (1580) and 'Astrophel' (1591), to Milton's 'Lycidas', Shelley's 'Adonais' (1821, in memory of his fellow-poet John Keats) and Matthew Arnold's 'Thyrsis' (1867).

The pastoral convention had been revived, and had come strongly into favour, in the Renaissance ('re-birth') in Europe, that period when the literature of the classical world of Greece became known again. From about the fourteenth century onwards, classical literature with its often delightful and fanciful imagination, and its many stories about the ways in which the lives of the gods and humans mixed and intertwined, came back again. The writers, especially of Italy, began to write in classical forms, and even seemed to acquire a classical way of looking at things, were 're-born' as it were with classical imaginations. European countries, with Italy as always in the lead, began to want and to create a literature written in their own language. It was natural for Italy, the inheritor of the two great classical civilisations, to be the leader and chief centre of the movement, and to turn to the works of Greece and Rome for inspiration.

Of course pastoral was a minor literary form, occupying a humble place after the great classical forms of tragedy – although this was not much revived in the Renaissance – and above all of epic. (All the Western European countries in turn tried epic; their poets tried to write odes and lyrics too.) And in the Renaissance, a quite new element came into pastoral, and a surprising one: the element of satire. (Satire is a literary form in which a subject – individuals, manners, society itself – is attacked and belittled, sometimes by making it comic and laughable, sometimes by ridiculing it with varying degrees of apparent hatred.) The Roman satirists on the whole preserved a distinct distance from the pastoralists, although some traces of complaint appear in some eclogues. The satirical element, which was almost entirely to do with religion, probably came into pastoral quite naturally once the connection between shepherd and flock was seen in religious terms. In the New Testament, Christ is called 'the good shepherd', and he himself referred to the feeding of his flock. This gave added strength to the idea that pastoral presented pictures of ideal and virtuous living. But once you moved from thinking of Christ, the Son of God, as a shepherd, and applied the metaphor of the shepherd and his flock to the priests and ministers of the Church, it was but a short step to see that there could be good and bad shepherds, good and bad priests. And so satire entered the pastoral form; originally in the *Eclogues* 6 and 7 of the Italian Petrarch (1304–74). It followed the method of indignant scorn rather than laughter.

The ecclesiastical satire in 'Lycidas' occupies only twenty-two lines (110–31), and to some it still seems odd and discordant. But King was a priest, and Milton had thought of being one. Religion mattered greatly to Milton. In any case he was idealistic enough to dislike insincerity, slackness and corruption in ministers of religion. He was probably most influenced here by Edmund Spenser, who wrote several satirical eclogues, attacking just this sort of thing, as well as the danger from the growth of Roman Catholicism – presented as in 'Lycidas' as wolves in the May and September eclogues – in *The Shepheardes Calender*. The satirical attack in this passage in 'Lycidas' is meant to reinforce the idea of how good a priest has been lost by King's death. It also introduces a strong, even harsh element of contrast into the poem, and, although it is itself, like everything else in the poem, presented in the allegorical terms of pastoral poetry, it seems to make the poem more real, since it points to actual dangerous abuses in the life of the time.

We may expect to find in a pastoral elegy the following:

(1) The poem usually begins with the poet calling on the Muses (but he may instead or as well call on other figures from Classical mythology – gods or nymphs, for example).

(2) Trees, woods, flowers – all nature – are shown as grieving over the death of the shepherd.

(3) Nymphs or other guardians of the dead shepherd are asked where they were when he died.

(4) There is a procession of mourners, and of others paying respect to the dead shepherd-poet.

(5) His virtue is praised.

(6) The transitoriness or brevity of human life is pointed out.

(7) The poet questions the justice or rightness of such a virtuous man's being killed untimely, but goes on to find justification in faith.

(8) Perhaps mourners come and place flowers on the grave or hearse, which gives the poet opportunity to describe and list flowers.

(9) Finally, the elegy ends with hope, and with assurance that the dead poet, for his virtue and worth, has been taken up by the gods or gone to Heaven, and general consolation is drawn from this.

You will see that this is almost a description of 'Lycidas'. It has, however, missed out the satirical section, which is a late Renaissance addition to the typical ingredients. It has also missed out the conclusion of 'Lycidas'. In this (lines 186–93), Milton steps outside the convention, and writes in the third person about the poet who has written the elegy for Lycidas, describing how he has sung of Lycidas and how, having finished now at evening, he rises, draws his mantle about his shoulders and prepares for a new life tomorrow. This is Milton, ending the poem as he began it, by thinking of himself. He began – in the guise of the elegist – by regretting not only the death of King, but that his death forces him to take up writing again before he is quite ready to do so. (It seems that he had not written any English poetry in the three years before 'Lycidas' was called for, except to revise *Comus*. He was in retirement in the country at Horton, 'reading through the Greek and Latin authors' as he wrote in *Defensio Secunda*). He ends by referring to the new hopes and expectations of the elegist – himself. It is also a statement that, if the poem is an elegy for the death of a poet, it is also an affirmation of the continuing life of poetry itself.

This, and other references in the poem, have led some to think that really Milton is thinking more about himself than about the dead Fellow of Christ's College, Cambridge. His career so far had been very similar to that of Edward King: they had been at the same college; both were poets; both had had thoughts of entering the Church, and King would have had to take Holy Orders to become a Fellow. We may suppose that King, like Milton, was a serious and idealistic man. Naturally, the untimely death of a friend and contemporary makes a man think about his own life. Milton in 'Lycidas' pauses to wonder whether it is worth while to devote your life to the noble pursuit of learning and the practice of serious poetry if at any moment Fate may take you off (lines 64–84); and implies an affirmative answer in the intervention of Phoebus about everlasting 'fame in Heaven'.

All sorts of other interpretations have been made, of varying complexity: that Milton was torn between the rival claims of Protestant conviction and Renaissance humanism (though he harmonises them beautifully); that the conflict is between a pagan and a Christian world-view (but is there any conflict?); that the conflict is between the ideal pastoral world and the real world; that the basic image of the poem, the image of Orpheus, poet-prophet killed by wild women, means that the subject of the poem is the destruction of human wisdom and art by barbarism (but this is to give undue prominence to that image, and so to falsify the meaning of the poem). A more consistent image is that of water and of things associated with water; naturally enough, since Lycidas was drowned in the sea, water-nymphs and gods of water, rivers and the sea are invoked, and tears in any case naturally accompany grief.

You should remember that this is a conventional poem. Milton was one of many who were asked to contribute to the commemorative volume. It contained twenty-three Latin and Greek and thirteen English pieces. We do not know that he was a particularly close friend of King. We do not have to suppose that it was all deeply heartfelt. No; Milton was still preparing himself to be a poet. Asked to contribute, he chose to write a completely conventional pastoral elegy, successfully including in it all the elements found in classical and in Renaissance pastoral elegy. We are not to suppose he was in tears as he wrote.

What, then, is the point of pastoral elegy? How sincere does it have to be? But how can you measure sincerity? We have to remember that poetry in the Renaissance was much more formal than it is now. The poet did not spend his time investigating his own soul or instincts. He was not, on the whole, writing of himself, or expressing personal emotion. He was much more like an artist: his task was to create an interesting, beautiful object. This is not to say that the poet did not feel, or that he could not make his reader feel, any emotion; far from it. The formal organisation of a funeral, wedding or any other religious ceremony does not mean that no emotion is felt by the actors or participants or by the onlookers. Every ritual or ceremony of that kind is reminiscent of every other one. The emotion created may be the greater not only because it re-enacts things experienced before but also because of the very formality of the presentation. That is the principle behind the organising of public grief or mourning or celebration in all countries at all times. Further, in the matter of grief, there is comfort given to the mourners by the sense of age-long repeated ritual. And there is perhaps still more comfort given by the formality, which sets their personal grief at a distance, making it more bearable, making it a little more like 'art' than like 'life', yet at the same time asserting that this death and sorrow are an inescapable part of human life, shared by every human being.

In all this Milton succeeds admirably. The grief *is* 'distanced'; it *is* ritualised; it *is* seen as part of the general human reaction to death and bereavement. And who will say it is without emotion? You ought to read again, slowly, carefully and aloud, lines 8–14; 37–49; 142–51, noting the falling cadences, the interspersed short lines, the simplicity of utterance. Then read lines 172–81, which, of course, because they are celebrating triumph, not sorrow, are buoyant, with a lifting, upward movement, and a slow and swelling grandeur; for Lycidas 'is not dead' but is 'mounted high' and lives now with the saints in Heaven.

Style and verse

The poem consists of eleven verse-paragraphs of varying length and varying rhyme-scheme. It is mostly in ten-syllabled five-stress lines, with a few six-syllabled three-stress lines interspersed. Each verse-paragraph ends with a rhyming couplet, and this, together with the use of the short lines, was influenced by the Italian *canzone* form, especially as freely adapted by Milton's great predecessor Edmund Spenser. Milton has, in fact, brilliantly changed the Italian seven- and eleven-syllabled lines to ten- and six-syllabled ones. He derived also from Spenser the use of English dialect words ('rathe', daffadillies', and so on) and Spenserian country words and usages from his pastoral collection, *The Shepheardes Calender* (1579). Probably he also learned from these eclogues the straightforward simplicity of diction, unusual in him, and a high proportion (eighty per cent) of words of Anglo-Saxon, not Latin, origin.

Samson Agonistes

You should read the account of the life and exploits of Samson in the Bible, Judges 13–16, but here is a summary of what you need to know of the events before Milton's poem begins.

Samson was a Hebrew, and came from one of the tribes of Israel, the tribe of Dan, which lived in a valley to the west of Jerusalem. He was the son of Manoa, who had been childless and prayed to God for children. The angel of God had come to Manoa's wife, told her that she would conceive, and that the son born to her would 'begin to deliver Israel out of the hand of the Philistines' who had long oppressed the Israelites. He was to be brought up a Nazarite, sacred to God; his head was never to be shaved. Manoa had entreated God for further instructions, and the angel returned: the mother was not to touch any wine or strong drink, or to eat any unclean thing. Manoa had then sacrificed a kid, and the angel had ascended to Heaven in the flames of the altar fire.

We hear about this early in the poem. Milton does not give much space to Samson's marriage to the woman of Timnath, a Philistine, and only briefly mentions the slaying of the lion with his bare hands, the bees which swarmed in its carcase and the riddle he set. We learn of the deceit of the woman, but very little of Samson's revenges – killing the Thirty, smiting the Philistines 'hip and thigh with a great slaughter', and slaying a thousand of them with the only weapon that came to hand, the jaw-bone of an ass. Milton does not mention the episode of the setting fire to

Philistine cornfields by tying firebrands to the tails of three hundred foxes in pairs and turning them loose.

Samson in the Old Testament was clearly a kind of Hercules, a fabulous folk-hero of superhuman strength of whom improbable exploits were told. Naturally, Milton played down this fairytale, tall-story element in the source in order not to threaten the tragic seriousness he aimed at. He also played down Samson's relationships with women, making Dalila wife and not mistress and omitting the detail that it was after visiting a harlot that he took the gates of the city of Gaza and set them up at the top of a nearby hill. But he also omits the fact that Samson was a judge of Israel for twenty years, and that the theme of the Old Testament story is really revenge. Samson does not 'deliver Israel' in the biblical story, though he kills many Philistines, and 'the dead which he slew at his death were more than they which he slew in his life'.

When you turn from reading these chapters of the book of Judges (only one, Chapter 16, records the events Milton actually presented in *Samson Agonistes*) you will probably be amazed to find what a deep, serious and moving dramatic work the poet has made of them.

The first surprise, if you read Judges first, is to find that the story has been made into a sort of Classical tragedy. Milton prefaces *Samson Agonistes* with a brief essay on 'that sort of Dramatic Poem which is called Tragedy'. He begins by claiming that ancient tragedy has always been considered 'the gravest, moralest, and most profitable of all other poems'. He shows how the 'gravest' writers, philosophers, historians, biblical commentators and even Fathers of the Church have admired tragedy – and some have even written or tried to write it. Milton means by tragedy the classical Greek form, in verse, with a chorus of characters who ask questions, comment on the action and express some of the audience's likely responses to the unfolding situation on the stage, and representing a single tragic action happening within the space of twenty-four hours. It is true he writes that his work 'never was intended' for the stage, yet he has made it faithful to the Greek models, and it has frequently been successfully staged. Milton even follows the detailed organisation of a tragedy as defined by Aristotle in his *Poetics*. The summary shows the various parts of a tragedy, as followed by Milton from Aristotle's model.

Milton thought quite early in his career, at least as early as 1639, when he was thirty-one, of writing a tragedy. In a notebook, now known as the 'Cambridge MS' [Manuscript], he wrote down lists of possible subjects for future writing. As well as a list of characters for a drama on the Fall of Adam, there are listed other subjects from the Old Testament including four on events in the life of Samson from the book of Judges. Milton had a constant desire to write great serious literature, which would teach religion and morality: indeed, he thought that was his calling and duty in life. He wrote in *The Reason of Church Government* (1642), at the beginning of the second part, an autobiographical section about his literary aims. They included the possibility of an epic like the classical epics *or* 'a brief model' of an epic on the book of Job, and there is something of the epic suffering and endurance of Job in the drama of Samson. In the book of Judges there are no visitors to the imprisoned Samson, but in the book of Job the suffering hero is visited by three friends. They come to condole, and they stay to discuss the whole situation and God's purpose and the reasons for suffering – a function chiefly exercised by the Chorus in *Samson Agonistes*.

You can see, then, that we have in *Samson Agonistes* an Old Testament tale of a hero enduring punishment and pain. It is of course a Hebraic story of suffering and vengeance. Yet this is told by Milton in the form of a Classical tragedy. At first sight this might seem strange, and there has been much discussion of whether the poem is in fact Hebraic or Greek in spirit, but there is no difficulty here. Greek tragedy of heroic suffering and Old Testament tales of dedication and endurance are not so far apart, even in time of composition. Both take it for granted that there is a world beyond this world, a spiritual world as well as the material world we live in; and that it is controlled by some great divine power, Hebrew God or Classical gods; and that human life contains pain and suffering. Yet, of course, there is a distinction. The Hebraic God is above all concerned for his people, the Jews. He is all-powerful, demanding, sometimes threatening, sometimes cruel, but always he cares for the destiny of the Chosen Race. The classical gods are indifferent: the destiny they control is bleaker.

Milton chose to write this Old Testament story in the form of a Classical tragedy: a single action finally resolved by a great *peripeteia*, a reversal of fortunes. His Jewish hero fitted well into the Greek scheme of things on account of his fatal flaw or weakness. The Greek *hubris*, or pride, which arouses the antagonism of men and gods, is very like Samson's sin of pride, to the Christian the most significant of the seven deadly sins.

But there are differences. Samson is tempted in a number of ways; resisting temptation he grows in moral strength; and the conclusion, although tragic in the human scale, is also a triumph, and his reward is salvation. The Greeks are not so explicit, not even Sophocles in *Oedipus at Colonus* – with which, incidentally, *Samson Agonistes* has most in common: the blind and suffering hero is called on in turn by three persons who each represent an influence or pull to draw or tempt Oedipus back into the world from his resigned acceptance of his fate and punishment. Samson is visited by his father, his wife and a Philistine champion, each coming with a proposal which, if accepted, would in one way or another hold him back from the fulfilment of God's purpose.

Manoa wants to pay whatever ransom is necessary to free his son from the pain and degradation of imprisonment. This Samson rejects: he wants to pay in full by suffering for his criminal folly in betraying God's holy secret to his wife. This defiant acknowledgement of faults is the first stage in his regeneration, even though Samson is still in a state of self-reproachful despair. The Chorus recognises this, commenting on the need for faith in accepting the blows of Fate, and asserting that Patience is 'the truest fortitude'. His wife Dalila offers a similar temptation, but with the solace of sex and feminine care added to the proposal to solicit Samson's release. But he is not to be deceived yet again by her. Another stage of his regeneration has been reached, for he has shown a return of his old powerful energy, and the passive despair of the earlier scenes is replaced by a positive spirit. The Middle Ages would have found in this scene a victory by the hero over concupiscence (lust) and sloth as well as despair. The episode ends with the Chorus again commenting on the heroic element in patient endurance. The re-kindled energy of Samson is further fired by the contemptuous taunting of Harapha, in the course of which he declares his 'trust in the living God', challenges the giant to single combat and threatens to attack him there and then. The Chorus gladly notes the resurgence of energy and strength in him. The total effect of the three visits is shown after Samson has at first rejected the Officer's demand, with the lines:

> '. . . I begin to feel
> Some rousing motions in me which dispose
> To something extraordinary my thoughts'

and from this time he feels the spirit of God within him, impelling him forward – and, as we know, to his final, tragic glory.

We can see how the Chorus helps to achieve this development. It is another sign of Milton's wisdom in telling his chosen story from the Old Testament in the form of Greek tragedy. It was necessary to have some person or persons to whom Samson could talk. Having a chorus on stage throughout, and that a chorus of men of Samson's own tribe, sympathetic to him but not uncritical of his past doings or of his present emotional responses, was a most valuable device. It made the telling of past events acceptable as the story could come out gradually, bit by bit. Above all, it made it possible for Milton to show the development in Samson – towards faith in God's purpose and therefore to hope and renewed energy and ultimately towards salvation – as an emerging, deepening spiritual process, thoroughly investigated and commented on by the Chorus.

Milton wrote that he did not intend *Samson Agonistes* for the stage. Yet it has considerable dramatic impact, when staged, not only because of the dramatic scenes of confrontation but also because of the dramatic irony running through it. From the beginning Samson (and the audience) knows that God had a purpose for Samson. Neither Samson nor any character in the piece knows how God's purpose, apparently long ago frustrated, will be worked out. So there is tension. Then each encounter has its own drama and surprises, and cumulatively. The meeting with Dalila, with her subtle twistings and changes of approach, is more dramatic and intriguing than that with Manoa; and the encounter with Harapha is more rousing and theatrical still. The drama reaches a climax with the offstage noise, and the arrival of the breathless and appalled messenger to tell the tale of woe and triumph. Finally, the play ends in acceptance and calm.

The inner drama in *Samson Agonistes*, stronger than in any Greek tragedy, is also in fact, although it is only concerned with movements of the mind, dramatic. Certainly, that is what Milton intended. The drama is the drama of the struggling champion and contestant. From the beginning we know of Samson's *perplexity* – what is to become of the prophecy that he was destined for some great deed, now that he is blind, humbled, and a prisoner? Before long, he begins to look inward for the fault or cause, and finds it in his *pride* and *folly*. This marks the beginning of a process of *penitence*. Discussion with his father, and much more significantly, with the Chorus, establishes this, and leads on to the two remaining major ideas: that, as a prisoner, he can do little, and so must dedicate himself to *patience*, awaiting the revelation of God's purpose. And this itself is developed into understanding that *fortitude*, patient, faithful endurance, accepting God's will without chiding, may be as heroic as great deeds. Perhaps above all there is the idea that one must simply wait and trust: God's purpose *will* be worked out. Blind Milton must often have felt this, and one should not underestimate the appeal of the subject to him on these grounds. Admittedly, there was no hint of Milton's coming blindness, as far as we know, when he jotted down the list of Samson plots in about 1638 or 1639. What, then attracted him to the subject? It was the ideas of heroism, temptation, punishment, penitence, epic endurance, salvation. It might have been also the idea of betrayal by or susceptibility to women. If it was begun before the Civil War, which is possible, the apparent failure of his marriage within two months, which occurred in 1642 – his wife returned to him in 1645 – and which led to the writing of the divorce pamphlets in 1643 and 1644, may have prompted him to start it. And as early as September 1644 he had written that he had begun to notice his sight beginning to fail. Certainly, by 1671, when it was first published, the poor man had been blind for nearly twenty years, and some of the power of the presentation of Samson's bitterness must come from Milton's own suffering.

The other preoccupations of Samson, the sense of divine calling and of purpose frustrated, and the disillusionment with women and with marriage, had their real-life counterparts. The Milton who felt called to a life of dedication to serious moral writing and the Milton who believed in and supported the reforming cause in England and who served the reforming government as Secretary for the Foreign Tongues (Latin Secretary for Foreign Affairs to the Council) felt tragically frustrated and betrayed when his hopes for republicanism and reformed religion faded, and especially when what he thought of as the tyranny of the Stuart monarchy was restored in 1660. And though his second and third marriages may not have been particularly unhappy, his domestic life and his relations with his daughters were always disappointing, and much of his writing, especially in *Samson Agonistes* and *Paradise Lost* shows contempt and dislike for women.

Milton was deeply conscious of the fallen state of man. Most of his work deals either with the moral dangers and temptations of the world or with the endless struggle which man must wage to keep his moral and spiritual self stronger than his passions and instincts. *Samson Agonistes* offers an excellent example of both, stronger and more intellectual than in *Comus*, more concentrated than in *Paradise Lost.*

With what subtlety, skill and certainty Milton has elevated the barbaric, wild and amorous 'superman' hero of the book of Judges into a figure of tragic resignation, seriously reviewing the course of his life, honestly analysing his mistakes and his defects of character, and, in the end, only wanting the fulfilment of God's will, and going out glowing with recovered strength and certainty to achieve it.

Style and verse

Samson Agonistes is written mostly in a mixture of regular and of extremely irregular blank verse. The partly-rhymed lyric verse which some writers claim is used for the choruses, and which is said to be freely based on both the lyric of classical Greece and Rome and on the Italian *canzone* form, does not seem to exist. To be sure, the speeches of the Chorus are in lines of daringly irregular length, and so are parts of some of Samson's speeches. In lines 86–109 of his first speech, for example, the five-stress blank verse line suddenly gives way to some two-stress six-syllable lines:

> The sun to me is dark
> And silent as the Moon,
> When she deserts the night ...

before reverting to the full ten-syllabled blank verse line:

> Hid in her vacant interlunar cave.

The three lines are not rhymed, but they are certainly lyrical. Clearly Milton wanted, and achieved, variety. He also achieved here a quietly singing quality, to express more poetically and emotionally the idea of sadness and deprivation. A few lines later in the same speech, he again changes from blank verse to this six-syllabled, two-stress line for two lines, not very lyrical ones:

Life in captivity
Among inhuman foes.

There hardly seem to be any passages of real lyric verse, such as we find in Spenser or in *Comus*. It would be safer to say simply that *Samson Agonistes* is written chiefly in unrhymed verse with very great variation in the length of the line. The lines tend to shorten and become more 'singing' or lyrical when more emotion is to be expressed, but, after all, here it is speech above all that Milton is writing. The greatest amount of rhyming comes in the last fourteen lines, the final speech of the Chorus, which is in sonnet form except for variable syllabling.

There is also great flexibility in stress and syllabling. Many lines in fact run to many more syllables than ten, even than twelve, but usually the number of stresses is easily kept to the norm of five by the use of elision, by which syllables are run over or slurred ('the' often becomes 'th'' and attaches itself to the vowel opening the next word; syllables are silently dropped). In any case there are very many 'feminine endings' – in which a longer line on the page does not sound longer when spoken for it ends with an unstressed syllable or even more than one.

The style of *Samson Agonistes*, while containing much of Latin vocabularly, syntax, inversions and so on, yet gives an overall impression of plainness and directness. This is partly because Milton has sparsely used classical references and epic devices (properly, as this is not an epic and is not set in the classical world), partly because there is less imagery anyway, for the verse is explaining, discussing, arguing, rather than describing. However, some have seen extensive use of marine imagery, and considerable use of bird, animal and even flower imagery. It certainly exists, but it is hardly strong or patterned enough for any theory to be built up about it.

What may be said is that the style and expression of *Samson Agonistes* are extremely effective. We feel that the speeches are convincing. They often seem (even like Shakespeare's, although they are not in any way Shakespearean) to have the casual, rather wandering, sometimes almost incoherent quality of real speech. Sometimes, perhaps often, the quality of the speech seems admirably to characterise the speaker, whether it be the despairing, self-reproachful tone of Samson's early speeches, the sympathetic but honest responses of the Chorus, Dalila's soft, blandishing tone changing to defiant malice, or Harapha's curt contempt.

Part 4

Hints for study

General points

You should, in your reading of poetry, from time to time read aloud. This is particularly helpful in the case of a poet like Milton, whose verse is carefully contrived to be musical and sonorous. You cannot get the full impact without the sound. Reading aloud to yourself – or classroom reading aloud – will bring out the form and musicality of the poems, their grandeur and flow, their lightness and their strength, their seriousness and their beauty. It will demonstrate their variety, the skill with which the poet varies from stanza to stanza, as a composer does in music. It will also greatly help to bring out their meaning. In addition, you will get to know the poems better. A further point: Milton's poetry was generally 'public', not private; it is addressed to an audience.

You should, then, first of all read as much of a poem aloud as you can. If it is a comparatively short poem, like the 'Nativity Ode' or 'Lycidas', read all of it aloud. Do not, at first reading, worry at all about things you do not immediately understand. Read aloud, slowly and clearly, as if to an audience, trying to let your voice fall into the natural rhythms and emphases of the lines. You will see that the 'Ode' is written in stanzas, with a repeating pattern of long and short lines. Pause between the stanzas briefly. When the short lines come, speak them lightly; you will find they often have a natural lilting or dancing rhythm. 'Lycidas' is not written in stanzas, but in a number of verse-paragraphs. Treat them as long stanzas, reading right through a paragraph without stopping, then pausing, and then going on to the next.

Having done that, you will probably find that you have understood much more than you expected. Then go back to the beginning, and read through again, this time stopping where there is something you do not understand and consulting the notes in this volume. Only then should you read the summary and commentary in these Notes. It is much better to try to make contact with the poem yourself. If you read the summary and commentary first, you will be seeing the poem, when you come to read it, at second hand. You will have lost the pleasure and the satisfaction of personally discovering its meaning and worth. With a poem like the 'Nativity Ode' or 'Lycidas', and certainly with long poems like *Comus* and *Samson Agonistes*, you should at the second reading write a summary in note form as you go along. It should be brief. A long

summary is not a summary at all. At this stage, too, you ought to make
notes of anything that particularly strikes you or pleases you: a vivid
phrase, a pleasing or moving cadence or rhythm, a memorable simile or
exciting metaphor, a phrase echoing a phrase you have met elsewhere or
a borrowing or imitation of another poet. All of these will help you to
build a basis of understanding and enjoyment of the poem. They will
also provide you with useful material for your essays.

Thoroughly get to know the poem and everything about it. If it is
based on a story or another work which is available, read that as well.
For instance, you should read the chapter in Judges from which Milton
took the story of *Samson Agonistes*. You should look at the Spenser
passages from which Milton took ideas for *Comus*. You should try to
read some of the elegies or translations of them mentioned above in
connection with 'Lycidas'.

You will probably not be able to remember all the notes, but you
should have discovered by now which notes are likely to matter most.
For example, in the case of the 'Nativity Ode', although you may not
need to remember in exact detail everything about the pagan gods, you
should be able to distinguish the Greek and Roman ones from those of
Egypt and Asia Minor.

In general, in studying Milton, you must know about the chief figures
of Greek and Roman mythology, about the biblical figures he refers to,
and something about the forms of *elegy*, *masque* and *tragedy*. The first
part of these Notes includes a lot of information about the religious and
political history of Milton's time: you should know a certain amount of
this, especially about Puritanism, Presbyterianism and the Civil War in
England.

You should also read some of Milton's other works, apart from those
set for special study, so that you can understand the place of the set texts
in Milton's development and in relation to his other work. Intelligent
comparing and contrasting is a very good way of bringing out the
quality and significance of a poem or a poet's work.

Preparing for examinations

In revising for an examination, you should not spend time reading all
through your old essays or class work. (You may, however, find looking
at old essays will produce some quotations for use in the examination.)
Do not try last-minute reading of critical works, either. What you want
to have uppermost in your mind when you go to write the examination is
the poems of Milton. Try to see the poems quite freshly. Go to the
examination room with a really deep knowledge of the *texts*, not with a
jumble of critics' opinions and some half-remembered fragments of
your own old essays.

Try to go to the examination eager to write about Milton, and determined to enjoy it. Do not go resentfully or anxiously. If you know your text well, and if you read the question very carefully, making sure you do what the examiner is asking and nothing else, and keeping to the question, you should have nothing to fear. The examiners want to know what you know, think and feel about the poems: they are not trying to catch you out or make you reveal ignorance. But they do not want you simply to put down as much as you can remember of Milton's lines, or about his life; they want your thoughts about and responses to the poetry, defined by the questions they set.

Writing essays and examinations

When preparing an essay, quickly summarise what you want to say, and repeatedly ask yourself 'What am I trying to say, wanting to tell them?' Sketch out the main lines of three or four paragraphs in note form. Jot down any quotations or references which support your argument. (You will find it helpful, in initial reading, to mark passages of particular interest, and to learn some of them by heart if you are required to write essays in class or in examinations from memory without being able to consult the text. Even if you are allowed to consult texts, learning by heart is still to be recommended. You may waste a great deal of time searching though a text for suitable quotations while you are actually supposed to be writing an essay.)

In examinations, read carefully – and calmly – through the whole paper, lightly marking questions you might want to do. Then go back again, and decide on the question or topic which most appeals to you and which you feel most capable of writing on, and write that essay first. Decide at the beginning how you are going to divide up the time available to you, allowing more time for the essay or essays you feel most happy about tackling.

On some rough paper, after reading the question again, jot down the topics of major interest that it suggests. Each of these will give you subject matter for one paragraph. When you jot them down, also put down any related ideas and any quotations which spring to mind. Then look at these notes, look back at the essay-question again to make sure all your notes really are relevant, and then (if they *are* relevant) put them in the most suitable order. You now have the whole plan of your essay, and with it beside you can begin to write. You will probably need three or four points; they, together with a brief introductory and a brief concluding paragraph, will give you five or six paragraphs, which is what you should aim at in an examination.

Do not waste time writing out the essay-question in full, or writing an opening sentence repeating what it says. Your opening paragraph should show that you are aware of the implications and the complexity of the question, and should outline the approach you are going to take. Try to illustrate every stage of your argument. If you cannot accurately remember the appropriate quotation, it is better to refer to it ('The writer says in effect that . . .') and then put it in your own words, rather than to write down an inaccurate, ill-remembered fragment. Your final paragraph may very briefly recapitulate the argument of your essay. If in your essay you are able to compare relevantly the work being discussed with another work by the same or another writer, either as you go along or in a final paragraph, you will impress the examiners not only with the width of your reading but with your mental power of selecting and comparing.

From time to time look back at the essay title, and keep asking yourself, 'Am I really answering the question, telling them what they have asked me to tell them?' It is only too easy to wander off the point. It is also easy to jump to conclusions about what a question, or a quoted sentence set for discussion, is really asking. There is an example of this in the specimen essay below about Johnson's remark about *Samson Agonistes*. Can you find it?

Specimen questions and answers

Much material for answering these questions is to be found in the commentaries and notes on the poems, and you are sometimes referred to those commentaries or to the notes.

Discuss the view that 'Lycidas' is an artificial poem, not portraying sincere grief. (Sometimes this sort of question takes the form of referring to Dr Johnson's complaint, of this poem, that 'Passion plucks no berries from the myrtle and ivy . . . where there is leisure for fiction, there is little grief'.)

You will have to consider two questions: 'How can sincerity be measured?' and 'Are not all poems artificial?' which immediately spring to mind. All poetry is in a sense artificial, or 'made by art'. In the sort of poetry which deals with emotion – and, of course, there is a whole body of poetry which does not – the poet may simulate emotions in words and metre. Whether or not he feels them himself is largely irrelevant, but it is to be doubted whether in the writing he fails to feel any emotion at all. What matters is that he tries to make us feel the emotion. In the case of an elegy it will be the emotions of grief and regret.

What leads the person who complains of 'Lycidas' to declare that real grief is not portrayed? Chiefly, it is the elaborate and formal way in which the poem is written. In 1637, people did not believe in nymphs or

Furies, gods and goddesses. Why, then, did Milton include them in the poem, making them play an important part in the structure and scene? Obviously it was because he was following the convention of classical elegy. (Here briefly discuss the elements common to Classical and much Renaissance elegy: see Commentary, pp. 75–8).

So in a sense, an elegy is a ritual celebration, paying tribute to the dead subject by celebrating his virtue or other qualities in established ways and forms, often repeated and well known. The celebration itself takes the minds of those present – or in the case of a poem its readers – away from regret over the loss to thinking admiringly of the dead. A negative emotion is replaced by a positive state of mind. This does not mean that real grief does not exist.

However, as readers we are entitled to ask if the poem does in fact move us. 'Lycidas' is certainly not without emotion, although admittedly the grief is distanced, ritualised, seen as part of the general human reaction to death and bereavement. Here you need to look at some passages in the poem to show that emotion is aroused, and how it is done. The passages quoted in the Commentary on p. 79 will give you an idea.

Your conclusion might be that the question of sincerity is irrelevant, that the poem is an excellent and successful effort in a conventional form, and that the 'fiction' that Johnson writes of – the conventional materials of the poem – gives it its charm and structure. From this structure, Milton was able to make his elegy a fitting tribute to King, and within it, to discuss further topics: poetic vocation, fame and honour, the Christian assertion of reward in heaven, and even the state of the Church. So, while it is a successful elegy, its very artificiality enables it to be also much more than simply an elegy.

Show how Milton drew inspiration and strength from tradition.

This question could be answered in relation to 'Lycidas' by using, in expanded form, the material given in the previous Specimen question and in the Commentary. The best sort of answer, however, would be more general and examine more than one poem. While you could limit it to an examination of one work, it would obviously be better to deal with more than one. You could look at the masque tradition in relation to *Comus*, the tradition of tragedy in relation to *Samson Agonistes*, as well as the pastoral tradition in the elegy. Or you could examine his use of mythology, or of scripture. This specimen essay is limited to one small work, because other poems will be dealt with later. You could show, even in the case of a small work like 'On the Morning of Christ's Nativity', how Milton draws inspiration and strength from tradition in (a) form and (b) material.)

(a) The form is an English version of the Greek 'ode' or celebratory song. Although Milton does not try to follow in any exact way the metre or stanza form of the Greek 'ode' or of its Latin versions, the basic form of a sequence of very musical stanzas, skilfully varying long and short lines, is followed. The 'ode' was meant to be sung, and the 'singing', musical quality of Milton's stanzas emphasises this. (The introduction to the so-called 'Hymn' is in a more sober stanza form, not attempting to give the feel of a singing voice. It makes a straightforward contrast to what follows.) The ode form also allows Milton to use much imaginative and decorative material.

(b) The material derives from the not uncommon Renaissance nativity poems, especially Tasso's, with some valuable suggestions from Spenser's 'Hymne to Heavenlie Love'. Other English poets, including Jonson, Beaumont, Southwell, and Giles Fletcher, had written nativity odes and other poems on the subject. These poets had taken ideas gradually formed over centuries of thought about the event, and from centuries of religious poetry and art. It is not only a poem about ideas about the birth of Christ and the significance of that fact in the development of the Christian world, but also to some extent a very pictorial poem in traditional ways.

(Here you need to illustrate (i) the ideas about the birth and (ii) the pictorial element. For (i) you should introduce and discuss the idea that this extremely ordinary, simple, human event of a woman having a baby, had the most extraordinary impact on the future of the world. At the time, too, it had a tremendous immediate impact, as of some natural phenomenon; (for example, the sun holding back, the supernatural quiet and peace, the preternatural light, the singing of the Cherubim and Seraphim, the sudden frantic flight of all the gods and spirits of the pagan world). For (ii) you could look at, for example, stanzas xix (the pale-eyed priest), xx (the nymphs), xxi (the sweating marble), xxiii (the dismal dance about the furnace blue), xxiv (the sable-stoled sorcerers): all extremely economical and vivid.)

The traditions – the traditional form of a celebratory ode, the traditions about the physical impact on the world of the birth of Christ, the traditional view of the flight of the pagan gods, the traditions of pagan and other worship and ritual – are all made use of by Milton. He does not need to explain anything. That is the benefit and value of using traditional material: the poet can assume that, in general, his audience or readers are familiar with it. Quite small or minor devices in the poem can have large and certain effects. The originality lies in selection and juxtaposition. The chief strength perhaps comes from the fact that the writer can be concise and economical. This is particularly true of this 'Nativity Ode', which, in just over two hundred lines, many of them very short, encompasses a tremendous event and outlines its extraordinary, worldwide impact. A peculiar greatness of the poem is how the light, 'singing' quality of the ode and the mastery of traditional material enable Milton to make the great event, the greatest event in the history of the Christian world, that is the birth of God as a human to live on earth among humans, seem so simple, clear and compelling.

The impact of the poem on the reader is remarkable. Its deceptive simplicity is made possible by, and indeed is chiefly occasioned by, the traditional form and material.

Where can we find Milton in his poetry?

This is a large and interesting question. You should perhaps begin by pointing out the dangers of trying or expecting to find autobiographical reference in an author's works. This is especially so when you are dealing with a writer of the Renaissance, when the idea of personal self-expression, common enough since the Romantics, and extremely common in modern poetry, did not apply. Having uttered this caution, you could go on to say that Milton may be found a great deal in his poetry.

(In addition, he includes a great deal of autobiography and self-assessment in many of his prose works.) Five points of view follow:

(1) Milton had a strong conviction of the importance of the poet's calling. He dedicated himself quite early to the life of poetry, which meant also to him the life of learning. You could quote the passage (from *The Reason of Church Government urged against Prelaty*) in which he says he had come to feel 'that by labour and intent study (which I take to be my portion in this life) joined with the strong propensity of nature, I might perhaps leave something so written to after-times, as they should not willingly let it die'. He thought of the poet as one directly inspired by God, and that the poet had a duty to live a virtuous life and write poetry which taught right belief and good morals. Here you might quote from the *Apology for Smectymnuus*: 'he who would not be frustrate of his hope to write well hereafter in laudable things, ought himself to be a true poem; that is a composition and pattern of the best and honorablest things'. Naturally, then, he writes of inspiration and dedication, and often in relation to his own life and work. (Lines 64–84 in 'Lycidas' might be cited.)

(2) Milton was always a serious writer, and he did not conceal his convictions. Often in poetry he tries hard to sway the reader to his own moral viewpoint. (Lines 113–31 in 'Lycidas'; the whole central argument between the Lady and Comus about temperance, and the defence of chastity, also in *Comus*, are good examples.)

(3) Milton became much involved in political issues of his day. He wrote many prose tracts and pamphlets on public issues, on which he felt strongly, and it would be surprising if no signs appeared in his poetry. His political sonnets – 'On the Detraction', on Fairfax and Cromwell, 'On the Massacre' are small examples; his scorn of the Philistines and his contempt of and dislike for Dalila in *Samson Agonistes* are larger examples of his feelings towards political opponents and about women – the latter probably originally occasioned by his first wife's desertion. They certainly seem full of the pressure of strongly held opinions or prejudices.

(4) Milton's later disillusionment with the course of events embittered him, and his blindness understandably must always have been in the forefront of his mind. (Both disillusionment and blindness are major themes in *Samson Agonistes*.)

(5) In lighter and pleasanter vein, Milton may be seen in both 'L'Allegro' and 'Il Penseroso', companion-poems which describe different moods and interests, different types of man ostensibly, but which seem also to present different, but here not necessarily conflicting, aspects of his personality.

Here are five different ways, with references given to appropriate poems, of investigating the question: five paragraphs, perhaps, for your essay. However, if you wanted to strengthen the essay still more, and to devote some space to a detailed examination of one work, you could fix on either *Comus* or *Samson Agonistes*. In the case of the former, you could concentrate on the Lady's impassioned defence of chastity and arguments for temperance, and the supporting speeches by her brothers before the scene of her 'temptation' by Comus, which are obviously deeply felt views of Milton's own. Those parts of the prose *Apology for Smectymnuus* in which he develops his ideals of chastity and writes autobiographically should be looked at. In the case of *Samson Agonistes*, you could investigate in detail all the places where Samson condemns the Philistines, and also those in which he attacks the Israelites for supinely putting up with Philistine domination. These derive from his own strongly held views about the royal tyranny in England and also the Presbyterian tyranny (or, rather, intolerance), and also, after the Restoration, from his feeling that the people of England have betrayed the cause, in the end loving

> bondage more than Liberty,
> Bondage with ease than strenuous liberty

(lines 270–1)

You could also explore the many passages which deal with Samson's blindness; they must have been inspired by Milton's like misfortune.

Discuss the view that there is really no drama in *Samson Agonistes*. (This
sort of question sometimes comes in the form of an invitation to discuss
Dr Johnson's dictum that it has 'a Beginning and an End . . . but it must
be allowed to want [must be admitted that it lacks] a middle, since
nothing passes between the first Act and the last, that either hastens or
delays the death of Samson'.)

It would be sensible to begin by straightforwardly questioning whether
Dr Johnson was right. Is it actually true that 'nothing passes between the
first Act and the last'? What does actually happen? The answer is that
Samson, blind and in despair, is visited by a number of people, and
converses at intervals with a group of men, the Chorus. The
conversations with the Chorus investigate Samson's total situation, all
the events of the past, the predictions of his future great triumphant deed
(the nature of which is still unknown), and elements of his character.
With regard to the last, the Chorus is patient, supporting, sympathetic
and encouraging, while Samson himself bitterly chides himself for his
follies. Here is a clue to the 'action', the inner action, of the drama. You
might specially point this out, because Samson's clear understanding of
his mistakes and his repentance mark the beginning of his 'redemption'.
    The other visitants all in some way further the process of self-
realisation, self-criticism and so eventual restoration to God's will. You
should examine carefully what each visitant says and how Samson
responds. Manoa first comes, offering the possibility of a comparatively
easy way out of his captivity for Samson. What is Samson's response?
Next his treacherous wife Dalila comes deceivingly. Show the
significance of her proposals and of Samson's rejection of them. Do the
same with Harapha, the boastful giant and champion of the Philistines.
You will see that in quite different ways with their quite different
'temptations', they unintentionally test Samson. His growing mental
strength to resist them parallels the gradual return of his physical
strength.
    At this point return to the question of whether it is true that there is no
drama in *Samson Agonistes*. You could now ask the question which was
implied at the end of the first paragraph. You have discussed what
happens in the main body of the poem, but could it not be said to be only
'inner action'? It is not, apparently, very dramatic action in stage terms:
three different people come on and talk. (Yet there is some drama in the
conflict between each of them and Samson, and increasingly so.
Compare the bitter anger with Dalila with the scornful rage against
Harapha.) At this point, too, you could remind the reader that Milton
expressly wrote in his brief introductory essay that this 'work never was
intended' for the stage. You may have noticed that in these Notes it is
called a 'poem' or a 'drama', never a 'play'. Does the person who set this

essay, or Dr Johnson, make an obvious mistake in thinking in terms of dramatic stage action in a poetic drama? Is not Milton really – and rightly – more interested in 'inner action', in the religious argument, in Samson's repentance, moral strenthening, spirit of acceptance and regeneration, than in dramatic stage happenings?

Now, if you are tackling the Johnson quotation, you should look at it again carefully. What Johnson writes is not simply that the poem has no 'middle', but that what happens in the middle of the drama does not have any effect upon the character or fate of the hero, Samson: 'Nothing passes . . . that either hastens or delays the death of Samson'. Is this true? We have already shown the effect of the visiting temptations. They strengthened his sense of his own wrong past actions, showed him humbling himself before God and wanting above all in the future simply to do God's will. This moral regeneration means that God's spirit is beginning to work again within him. Consequently, when the final visitor (and 'temptation') comes in the shape of the officer who summons him to perform before the Philistines, Samson begins to feel that this marks the beginning of God's final purpose. So he accepts the order of the officer and goes off. If Johnson wanted strong or violent action *on stage*, as it were, then certainly he is right, and there is none. But surely he is wrong to expect or demand this, as the poem is one about an inner drama of spiritual development. In any case, in thinking of it as a stage-play, he is again at fault, for the model is Greek tragedy, in which no violent stage-action occurs.

A final paragraph might look at the dramatic speeches in the confrontations between Samson and his visitors. It could mention the sense of some impending great event which, running throughout the poem, communicates dramatic expectation. This expectation is fulfilled in the final two hundred lines, first when the Chorus rushes in and twice the dreadful sound is heard, and then, of course in the Messenger's long speech describing the great event – when Samson pulled down the temple upon the Philistines, dying, himself, in the ruins. So there is plenty of drama in the poem, even if there is not much 'stage-action'.

Part 5

Suggestions for further reading

The text

(a) *Complete*

BEECHING, H. C. (ed.): *The English Poems of John Milton* in modern spelling, with Reader's Guide to Milton, and Introduction by Charles Williams, World's Classics, Oxford University Press, London and New York, 1940. (the handiest edition).

BUSH, D. (ed.): *The Complete Poetical Works of John Milton*, Boston 1965; Oxford Standard Authors, Oxford University Press, London, 1966. (an excellent paperback edition)

PATTERSON, F. A. (ed.): *The Student's Milton*, Appleton, Century, Crofts, New York, 1933. (this volume contains the complete poetry and much of the prose).

HUGHES, M. Y. (ed.): *Complete Poems and Major Prose*, Odyssey Press, New York, 1957. (the best annotated edition).

CAREY, J. AND FOWLER A. (eds.): *The poems of John Milton* (Longmans Annotated English Poets), Longman, London & New York, 1968. (valuable annotated edition).

WRIGHT, B. A. (ed. text): AND CAMPBELL G. (introduction and notes): *Complete Poems*, Dent, London, 1980. (the latest complete edition, lightly annotated, in paperback).

(b) *Individual works*

PRINCE, F. T. (ed.): *'Comus' and other Poems*, Oxford University Press, London, 1968. (this includes the ode 'On the Morning of Christ's Nativity', 'L'Allegro', 'Il Penseroso', 'Lycidas' and the sonnets as well as *Comus*).

BULLOUGH, G. AND M. (eds.): *Milton's Dramatic Poems*, Athlone Press, London, 1958. (*Arcades, Comus* and *Samson Agonistes* comprehensively introduced and annotated).

PRINCE, F. T. (ed.): *Samson Agonistes*, Oxford University Press, Oxford, 1957.

These are the most useful and reliable editions, although there are others.

Background and general studies

HANFORD, J. H.: *A Milton Handbook*, 1926; 5th edition, revised Hanford & J. G. Taafe, Appleton, Century, Crofts, New York, 1970. (admirable, invaluable).

NICHOLSON, M. HOPE.: *A Reader's Guide to John Milton*, Thames & Hudson, London, 1964.

BUSH, DOUGLAS: *Mythology and the Renaissance Tradition in English Poetry*, W. W. Norton, New York, revised edition 1963. (excellent).

TILLYARD, E. M. W.: *The Miltonic Setting*, Cambridge University Press, Cambridge, 1938.

Criticism

BARKER, A. E. (ed.): *Milton: Modern Essays in Criticism*, Oxford University Press, New York, 1965.

CRUMP, G. M.(ed.): *Twentieth Century Interpretations of 'Samson Agonistes'*, Prentice Hall, Englewood Cliffs, New Jersey, 1968.

ELIOT, T. S.: *On Poetry and Poets*, Faber, London, 1957.

KERMODE, F. (ed.): *The Living Milton*, Routledge and Kegan Paul, London, 1960.

LOVELOCK, J. (ed.): *Casebook* on *'Comus'* and *'Samson Agonistes'*, Macmillan, London, 1975.

PATRIDES, C. A. (ed.): *Lycidas*, Holt, Rinehart and Wilson, New York, 1961.

THORPE, J. E. (ed.): *Milton Criticism: Selections from Four Centuries*, Rinehart, New York, 1950; Routledge and Kegan Paul, London, 1951.

The author of these notes

PETER BAYLEY is a graduate of University College, Oxford. He was for twenty-five years Fellow and Praelector in English of this college, and a University Lecturer in English. He then became Master of a newly founded college at Durham University, (Collingwood College) 1971-78, and then Berry Professor of English and Head of the Department of English at the University of St Andrews in Scotland, 1978-85. He is Professor Emeritus of St Andrews.

He has edited Book I (1966) and Book II (1965) of Spenser's *The Faerie Queene;* written *Edmund Spenser, Prince of Poets* (1971) and a York Handbook, *An A.B.C of Shakespeare* (1985); edited the Macmillan *Casebook on The Faerie Queene* (1977) and *Loves and Deaths* (1972), a selection of short stories by the great nineteenth-century novelists. He has also produced *British Council Recorded Seminars* on *Macbeth* and *Antony and Cleopatra.*

York Notes: list of titles

CHINUA ACHEBE
A Man of the People
Arrow of God
Things Fall Apart

EDWARD ALBEE
Who's Afraid of Virginia Woolf?

ELECHI AMADI
The Concubine

ANONYMOUS
Beowulf
Everyman

JOHN ARDEN
Serjeant Musgrave's Dance

AYI KWEI ARMAH
The Beautyful Ones Are Not Yet Born

W. H. AUDEN
Selected Poems

JANE AUSTEN
Emma
Mansfield Park
Northanger Abbey
Persuasion
Pride and Prejudice
Sense and Sensibility

HONORÉ DE BALZAC
Le Père Goriot

SAMUEL BECKETT
Waiting for Godot

SAUL BELLOW
Henderson, The Rain King

ARNOLD BENNETT
Anna of the Five Towns

WILLIAM BLAKE
Songs of Innocence, Songs of Experience

ROBERT BOLT
A Man For All Seasons

ANNE BRONTË
The Tenant of Wildfell Hall

CHARLOTTE BRONTË
Jane Eyre

EMILY BRONTË
Wuthering Heights

ROBERT BROWNING
Men and Women

JOHN BUCHAN
The Thirty-Nine Steps

JOHN BUNYAN
The Pilgrim's Progress

BYRON
Selected Poems

ALBERT CAMUS
L'Etranger (The Outsider)

GEOFFREY CHAUCER
Prologue to the Canterbury Tales
The Clerk's Tale
The Franklin's Tale
The Knight's Tale
The Merchant's Tale
The Miller's Tale
The Nun's Priest's Tale
The Pardoner's Tale
The Wife of Bath's Tale
Troilus and Criseyde

ANTON CHEKOV
The Cherry Orchard

SAMUEL TAYLOR COLERIDGE
Selected Poems

WILKIE COLLINS
The Moonstone
The Woman in White

SIR ARTHUR CONAN DOYLE
The Hound of the Baskervilles

WILLIAM CONGREVE
The Way of the World

JOSEPH CONRAD
Heart of Darkness
Lord Jim
Nostromo
The Secret Agent
Victory
Youth and *Typhoon*

STEPHEN CRANE
The Red Badge of Courage

BRUCE DAWE
Selected Poems

WALTER DE LA MARE
Selected Poems

DANIEL DEFOE
A Journal of the Plague Year
Moll Flanders
Robinson Crusoe

CHARLES DICKENS
A Tale of Two Cities
Bleak House
David Copperfield
Dombey and Son
Great Expectations
Hard Times
Little Dorrit
Nicholas Nickleby
Oliver Twist
Our Mutual Friend
The Pickwick Papers

EMILY DICKINSON
Selected Poems

JOHN DONNE
Selected Poems

THEODORE DREISER
Sister Carrie

GEORGE ELIOT
Adam Bede
Middlemarch
Silas Marner
The Mill on the Floss

T. S. ELIOT
Four Quartets
Murder in the Cathedral
Selected Poems
The Cocktail Party
The Waste Land

J. G. FARRELL
The Siege of Krishnapur

GEORGE FARQUHAR
The Beaux Stratagem

WILLIAM FAULKNER
Absalom, Absalom!
As I Lay Dying
Go Down, Moses
The Sound and the Fury

HENRY FIELDING
Joseph Andrews
Tom Jones

F. SCOTT FITZGERALD
Tender is the Night
The Great Gatsby

E. M. FORSTER
A Passage to India
Howards End

ATHOL FUGARD
Selected Plays

JOHN GALSWORTHY
Strife

MRS GASKELL
North and South

WILLIAM GOLDING
Lord of the Flies
The Inheritors
The Spire

OLIVER GOLDSMITH
She Stoops to Conquer
The Vicar of Wakefield

ROBERT GRAVES
Goodbye to All That

GRAHAM GREENE
Brighton Rock
The Heart of the Matter
The Power and the Glory

THOMAS HARDY
Far from the Madding Crowd
Jude the Obscure
Selected Poems
Tess of the D'Urbervilles
The Mayor of Casterbridge
The Return of the Native
The Trumpet Major
The Woodlanders
Under the Greenwood Tree

L. P. HARTLEY
The Go-Between
The Shrimp and the Anemone

NATHANIEL HAWTHORNE
The Scarlet Letter

SEAMUS HEANEY
Selected Poems

JOSEPH HELLER
Catch-22

ERNEST HEMINGWAY
A Farewell to Arms
For Whom the Bell Tolls
The African Stories
The Old Man and the Sea

GEORGE HERBERT
Selected Poems

HERMANN HESSE
Steppenwolf

BARRY HINES
Kes

HOMER
The Iliad
The Odyssey

ANTHONY HOPE
The Prisoner of Zenda

GERARD MANLEY HOPKINS
Selected Poems

WILLIAM DEAN HOWELLS
The Rise of Silas Lapham

RICHARD HUGHES
A High Wind in Jamaica

THOMAS HUGHES
Tom Brown's Schooldays

ALDOUS HUXLEY
Brave New World

HENRIK IBSEN
A Doll's House
Ghosts
Hedda Gabler

HENRY JAMES
Daisy Miller
The Ambassadors
The Europeans
The Portrait of a Lady
The Turn of the Screw
Washington Square

SAMUEL JOHNSON
Rasselas

BEN JONSON
The Alchemist
Volpone

JAMES JOYCE
A Portrait of the Artist as a Young Man
Dubliners

JOHN KEATS
Selected Poems

RUDYARD KIPLING
Kim

D. H. LAWRENCE
Sons and Lovers
The Rainbow
Women in Love

CAMARA LAYE
L'Enfant Noir

HARPER LEE
To Kill a Mocking-Bird

LAURIE LEE
Cider with Rosie

THOMAS MANN
Tonio Kröger

CHRISTOPHER MARLOWE
Doctor Faustus
Edward II

ANDREW MARVELL
Selected Poems

W. SOMERSET MAUGHAM
Of Human Bondage
Selected Short Stories

GAVIN MAXWELL
Ring of Bright Water

J. MEADE FALKNER
Moonfleet

HERMAN MELVILLE
Billy Budd
Moby Dick

THOMAS MIDDLETON
Women Beware Women

THOMAS MIDDLETON *and* WILLIAM ROWLEY
The Changeling

ARTHUR MILLER
Death of a Salesman
The Crucible

JOHN MILTON
Paradise Lost I & II
Paradise Lost IV & IX
Selected Poems

V. S. NAIPAUL
A House for Mr Biswas

SEAN O'CASEY
Juno and the Paycock
The Shadow of a Gunman

GABRIEL OKARA
The Voice

EUGENE O'NEILL
Mourning Becomes Electra

GEORGE ORWELL
Animal Farm
Nineteen Eighty-four

JOHN OSBORNE
Look Back in Anger
WILFRED OWEN
Selected Poems
ALAN PATON
Cry, The Beloved Country
THOMAS LOVE PEACOCK
Nightmare Abbey and *Crotchet Castle*
HAROLD PINTER
The Birthday Party
The Caretaker
PLATO
The Republic
ALEXANDER POPE
Selected Poems
THOMAS PYNCHON
The Crying of Lot 49
SIR WALTER SCOTT
Ivanhoe
Quentin Durward
The Heart of Midlothian
Waverley
PETER SHAFFER
The Royal Hunt of the Sun
WILLIAM SHAKESPEARE
A Midsummer Night's Dream
Antony and Cleopatra
As You Like It
Coriolanus
Cymbeline
Hamlet
Henry IV Part I
Henry IV Part II
Henry V
Julius Caesar
King Lear
Love's Labour Lost
Macbeth
Measure for Measure
Much Ado About Nothing
Othello
Richard II
Richard III
Romeo and Juliet
Sonnets
The Merchant of Venice
The Taming of the Shrew
The Tempest
The Winter's Tale
Troilus and Cressida
Twelfth Night
The Two Gentlemen of Verona
GEORGE BERNARD SHAW
Androcles and the Lion
Arms and the Man
Caesar and Cleopatra
Candida
Major Barbara
Pygmalion
Saint Joan
The Devil's Disciple
MARY SHELLEY
Frankenstein
PERCY BYSSHE SHELLEY
Selected Poems
RICHARD BRINSLEY SHERIDAN
The School for Scandal
The Rivals
WOLE SOYINKA
The Lion and the Jewel
The Road
Three Shorts Plays
EDMUND SPENSER
The Faerie Queene (Book I)

JOHN STEINBECK
Of Mice and Men
The Grapes of Wrath
The Pearl
LAURENCE STERNE
A Sentimental Journey
Tristram Shandy
ROBERT LOUIS STEVENSON
Kidnapped
Treasure Island
Dr Jekyll and Mr Hyde
TOM STOPPARD
Professional Foul
Rosencrantz and Guildenstern are Dead
JONATHAN SWIFT
Gulliver's Travels
JOHN MILLINGTON SYNGE
The Playboy of the Western World
TENNYSON
Selected Poems
W. M. THACKERAY
Vanity Fair
DYLAN THOMAS
Under Milk Wood
EDWARD THOMAS
Selected Poems
FLORA THOMPSON
Lark Rise to Candleford
J. R. R. TOLKIEN
The Hobbit
The Lord of the Rings
CYRIL TOURNEUR
The Revenger's Tragedy
ANTHONY TROLLOPE
Barchester Towers
MARK TWAIN
Huckleberry Finn
Tom Sawyer
JOHN VANBRUGH
The Relapse
VIRGIL
The Aeneid
VOLTAIRE
Candide
EVELYN WAUGH
Decline and Fall
A Handful of Dust
JOHN WEBSTER
The Duchess of Malfi
The White Devil
H. G. WELLS
The History of Mr Polly
The Invisible Man
The War of the Worlds
ARNOLD WESKER
Chips with Everything
Roots
PATRICK WHITE
Voss
OSCAR WILDE
The Importance of Being Earnest
TENNESSEE WILLIAMS
The Glass Menagerie
VIRGINIA WOOLF
Mrs Dalloway
To the Lighthouse
WILLIAM WORDSWORTH
Selected Poems
WILLIAM WYCHERLEY
The Country Wife
W. B. YEATS
Selected Poems

York Handbooks: list of titles

YORK HANDBOOKS form a companion series to York Notes and are designed to meet the wider needs of students of English and related fields. Each volume is a compact study of a given subject area, written by an authority with experience in communicating the essential ideas to students of all levels.

AN INTRODUCTORY GUIDE TO ENGLISH LITERATURE
by MARTIN STEPHEN

PREPARING FOR EXAMINATIONS IN ENGLISH LITERATURE
by NEIL MCEWAN

EFFECTIVE STUDYING
by STEVE ROBERTSON *and* DAVID SMITH

THE ENGLISH NOVEL
by IAN MILLIGAN

ENGLISH POETRY
by CLIVE T. PROBYN

DRAMA: PLAYS, THEATRE AND PERFORMANCE
by MARGERY MORGAN

AN INTRODUCTION TO LINGUISTICS
by LORETO TODD

STUDYING CHAUCER
by ELISABETH BREWER

STUDYING SHAKESPEARE
by MARTIN STEPHEN *and* PHILIP FRANKS

AN A·B·C OF SHAKESPEARE
by P. C. BAYLEY

STUDYING MILTON
by GEOFFREY M. RIDDEN

STUDYING CHARLES DICKENS
by K. J. FIELDING

STUDYING THOMAS HARDY
by LANCE ST JOHN BUTLER

STUDYING THE BRONTËS
by SHEILA SULLIVAN

STUDYING JAMES JOYCE
by HARRY BLAMIRES

ENGLISH LITERATURE FROM THE THIRD WORLD
by TREVOR JAMES

ENGLISH USAGE
by COLIN G. HEY

ENGLISH GRAMMAR
by LORETO TODD

STYLE IN ENGLISH PROSE
by NEIL MCEWAN

AN INTRODUCTION TO LITERARY CRITICISM
by RICHARD DUTTON

A DICTIONARY OF LITERARY TERMS
by MARTIN GRAY

READING THE SCREEN
An Introduction to Film Studies
by JOHN IZOD